Recognizing and Understanding China Series

Yuwen Li

Translated by Zhang Xingquan

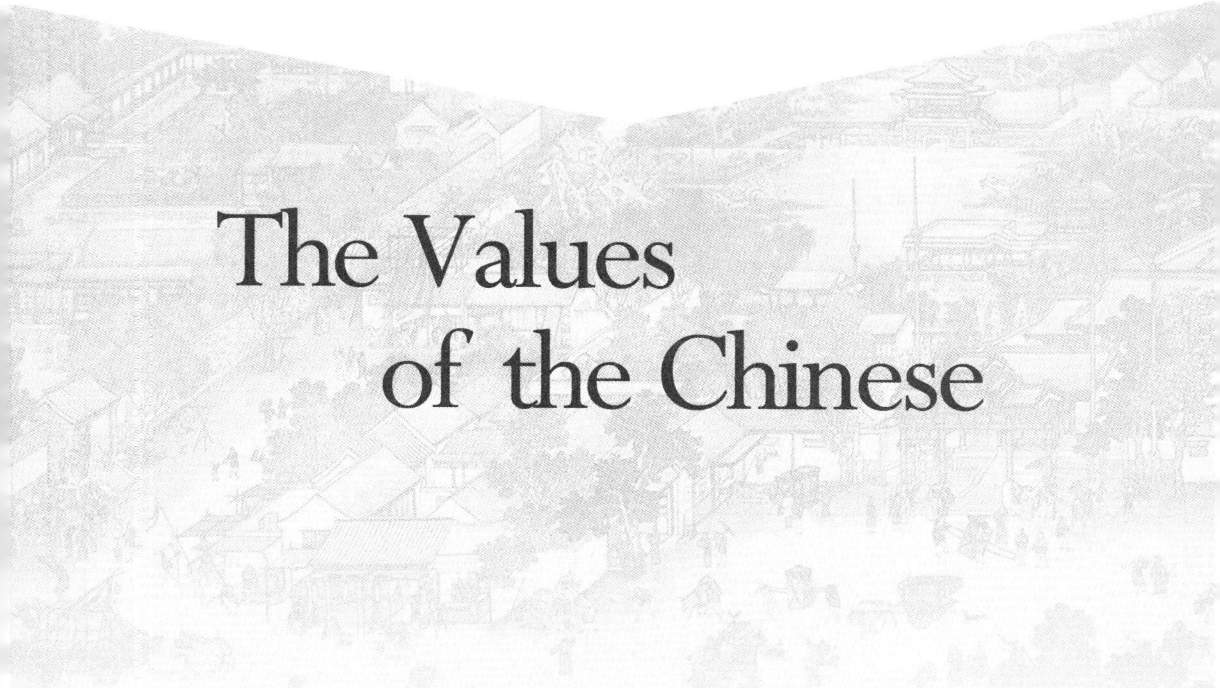

# The Values of the Chinese

China Renmin University Press

· Beijing ·

# Preface

What are values? What is the use of values? What is the relationship between values and me? What are the values of the Chinese like? And what are the contents of values? All these questions may flash into the readers' minds at their first sight of this book. But, with a little understanding of the purport and scope of this book, the reason why the Chinese have that kind of values perhaps will be the question that readers are most interested in before and in their reading of this book. As a matter of fact, the discussion of the issue about values is often regarded as a very serious academic topic or theoretical matter. And, when people discuss values, they usually interpret them through some abstract theories that make people feel very abstruse but still can not get rid of the fuzzy sense. Thus, the first impression of the word "values" left in people's mind is "vague and elusive". As a result, as regards such a topic about values, people tend to be reticent on it and avoid mentioning it. Even if talking about it, they often can not grasp its true meaning, or only touch on its superficial meaning like a dragonfly skimming the surface of the water. Nevertheless, in the scope of the knowledge of most people, or the scope seen or heard by them, there are still some works that talk about the values of the Chinese. Although these works do not mention them directly, values have permeated in their contents. Most of them are literary and historical works with light and easy style, which may inspire the readers and make them learn something, and this, is a common way to write about values. Such works are mostly derived from the authors' experiences, which are able to stand up to the test of their readers, and deserve the careful reflection in thought, the slow approaching in feeling, or the gradual closing in mind. There is quite a lot of such kind of works, even only counting those works that are still popular in recent years, and it is easy to give some examples: *The Spirit of the Chinese People* by Gu Hongming, *My Country and My People* by Lin Yutang, *The Character of the Chinese People* by Luo Jialun, *A Survey of the Chinese People* by Bo Yang, etc. However, this book you are reading is different from the above works, and in fact, the difference is precisely where the main idea of this book is, which, in a nutshell, is manifested in the following three aspects:

First, the difference in the direct title. Obviously, the theme of *The Values of the Chinese* is to deal with the values. As we know, values are different from the culture or the cultural personality, or even the personality spirit. They are standards, the core of culture, as well as the kernel of human spirit, and they are not neutral, but capable of making choices and judgments. Any kind of values embodies its value as well as the judgment of its value. However, value judgment is a very complex activity, which is related with people themselves, conditions people live in and the emotion, knowledge, quality and character of them. Since values permeate and manifest themselves in all aspects of people's life, production, study, work and contacts, it is hard to write about them, for which the very reason is that values exist everywhere at any time, in every person and every thing. For this reason, the works with the title of values that we usually see are either attributed to being too academic or too common. As for the former, the public may be unwilling to read or unable to understand it; while as for the latter, the public may find it hard to draw impressive and intuitive conclusions owing to its vacuous contents and spirit. Thus, obviously it is quite difficult to take a middle road between the two styles so as to organically combine academic study and common life. Despite this, I am willing to make some attempts to directly use values to title this book and transform some abstract and theoretical academic points of view into common and acceptable popular knowledge. Of course, this is the wish of the author, as for what the effect will be, it still remains to be judged by the readers.

Second, the difference in its subject. The subject of this book is the Chinese people, who are not the historical or traditional Chinese people, but the contemporary Chinese people. If we consider that the previous works show us an image of the Chinese people who live in the history or the tradition, then in this book, the image has been transferred to the contemporary era. The contemporary era here refers to the present time, that is, the current Chinese people. Of course, from a cultural perspective, the contemporary Chinese people can not be completely divorced from the shackles of traditional culture, for the culture is a special kind of life connector with the continuous and radiating nature, which can not be thoroughly separated and disconnected by the times. The great thinker Marx once compared the past ideological tradition to a "nightmare" on the brains of the living, believing that the ideology and spirit of the new age is developed in the inheritance and transformation of the old tradition. The values of the contemporary Chinese people are closely related with the values that were born in and continued from the Chinese history and tradition. So, this book intends to, on the one hand, find out the relationship between them, and on the other hand discover the creation and change in the values of the contemporary Chinese people. In short, this book aims to find the values of the Chinese that embody the modernity.

Third, the difference in its proposal of dimensions. The abovementioned works are a kind of works that research into values by means of concealing them in the people's way of life and survival in an indirect and implicit manner. This is where the merit of such kind of works lies. However, it is exactly because of this that the readers may easily get ambiguous conceptions from such kind of works, for when reading them, usually people can only vaguely grasp the visualized information about values, but will not explore the sources of the values or their precise manifestations. In academic circles, a lot of works that research into values tend to divide values into different levels and categories in accordance with the domestic or international academic consensus. Although there is not a unified classification at present, such a method of classification is undoubtedly the best way to refine, deepen and expand the research on values. The classification of values in this book is made on the basis of the combination of traditional and modern values and from the dimensions of life, politics, economy, culture and society, which mirror the overall view of the survival, living and life of the contemporary Chinese people from different sides. Although it may not be sufficient and perfect, it is able to take account of the reality of the existence and development of contemporary Chinese society. There's no doubt that the values reflected through such a classification of dimensions are exactly the survival values, political values, economic values, cultural values and social values of the Chinese.

Holding the spirit of exploration and conducting frank researches, seeking not to cover everything but to consider every detail, with such an attitude and spirit, we dedicate *The Values of the Chinese* to the contemporary Chinese and our friends who care about and wish to know about China, and we hope this book that depicts the spirit and values of the Chinese can vividly convey the true image of the Chinese people in respect of spiritual wishes and value pursuit in a fair and objective manner.

Yuwen Li

June, 2012

# Contents

# The Values of the Chinese

Chapter One

# A General Discussion and Evaluation of the Values of the Chinese

# 1

# A General Discussion and Evaluation of the Values of the Chinese

## 1. The Values and Their Appearance

What are values and their manifestations? From an academic perspective, it seems not difficult to answer this question. For those scholars who are engaged in theoretical research, they may easily find some rather academic definitions from the areas that they are proficient in, and can make an analysis of the definitions and quote the classics to support their arguments. Even for those scholars who were not familiar with this concept, they still can find a variety of explanations by consulting dictionaries or searching on the Internet. However, for the average people, especially the general public who do not specialize in research or are not used to acquiring knowledge from the Internet, the term "values" must be obscure and difficult to understand and be explained. If we simply define values by the use of a variety of definitions existing in different academic disciplines, for example, tell them "values" mean "the criteria that the subject applies for evaluating and choosing the objective things in accordance with their significance or importance to the subject itself and the society"[1], or "the criteria adopted by members of society to evaluate behaviors and matters, and to choose their desired goals among all a variety of possible targets"[2], or any other too academic definitions, it is certainly not easy for them to understand the true meaning of the concept. Ordinary people are different from scholars. They need the most concise, intuitive and succinct statement, because for them, they may even not try to carefully distinguish the nuances contained in various definitions of the concept, but just grasp the most straightforward explanation of some object. This is exactly the tastes and interests of the public, which is also the characteristic of the public in understanding a concept.

As a result, in order to make it concise and easily understandable and eliminate unnecessary academic debates and troubles in concept, we make some modifications to the definition of values that is most commonly used but still accurate, so as to popularize it as follows:

Values are the standards in people's minds, which represent the recognized value. With these standards, people can judge whether or not their own or others' words and deeds are important and accord with some of their own or universally recognized principles.

> Values are a standard for knowing and judging things.

In simpler words, values are a standard for knowing and judging things. In our daily life, we often express our views on some certain things or objects, evaluating whether or not they are important, correct, reasonable, advisable, true, good and beautiful, and whether they are consistent with our wishes and principles. The intrinsic yardsticks of value adopted by us to make evaluation in these respects are values.

For example, when a young passerby jumps into the pond to rescue a child from drowning without hesitation, some people may say it is foolish of him to risk his life to rescue the child; some would believe he is very brave, kind, beautiful in heart, and worth praising; and some others may be indifferent about it and stand aside without making comments. These three different ways of evaluation represent three different values. No matter what kind of evaluation people make, they all compare the external things, objects, and behaviors

Values: Behavior Guidance

with the standards of value inside their own mind, and then arrive at their own judgments. And no matter what kind of stance they take, they apply their personal values. But if the majority of people in the society or social institutions make a judgment on the behavior of the young people, then we say these people or social institutions are using the social values. In general, the values we talk about refer to the values of the majority of people in the society. Social values consist of individual values, but that is not to say they are equal to a hotchpotch of individual values, instead they are an organic and effective coupling of individual values, which are the unified and sublimated group values.

Values are very important for both individuals and groups. Talcott Parsons, a famous American sociologist, believes that values can be regarded as a factor like a yardstick in a conventional symbolic system, according to which, people make their own choice among a variety of alternative courses of action under certain circumstances. The famous *organizational behavior* scientist Robbins also said: "Values usually affect the attitude and behaviors of a person." "Values are very important for the study of organizational behavior, because they are the basis for the understanding of the attitude and motivation of employees. And they also have influence on our perception and judgment."[3] Popularly speaking, values are just like a beacon that guides the individual and groups' actions and illuminate the road along which people make value judgments and value choices. They are also like a balance that is weighing equipment used to measure the value as well as the right and wrong of certain objects, events, persons or behaviors. Under the guidance of values, people, in the face of choices, will know what should and what should not be done, what is and what is not reasonable, what kind of behavior is and is not favorable, etc. Therefore, just from the values of a person, we are able to judge his thought, sentiment, belief and behavior and know what the important value pivot that supports him in making his own decisions is, as well as what kind of value he believes in and what standards he adopts. It goes without saying that under the guidance of different values, a person may like and approve a matter, appreciate and recognize a behavior, and support and help another person, or he may take a completely opposite decision, opposing, criticizing and resisting the same matter, behavior and

Values are just like a beacon that guides the individual and groups' actions and illuminate the road along which people make value judgments and value choices.

person, instead. In brief, values are the intrinsic value that guides people to make choices and judgments, like the weights that control the direction and strength of the scales of the balance.

Scales of value

There are a variety of factors influencing the formation of people's values.

Since we have made clear about the importance of values, we still need to find out how values form. As regards this question, people may give different answers from different angles. For example, some people might say, "each place has its own way of supporting its own inhabitants", that is to say, geographical factors play a decisive role in the formation of values; some may hold "culture is personality", which means historical traditions and cultural factors play a dominant role in the formation of values; and some others would focus their attention on political, economic, or other factors, emphasizing their important role in the formation of people's values. In the field of research on modern social science, presently scholars' analysis of the formation of values tends to discuss it from the perspective of cultural anthropology and social psychology, which has almost become the most popular point of concern in the current interpretation of the issue of values. The researches on values from cultural anthropology and social psychology put emphasis on the analysis of people's psychological perception, emotional acceptance and moral acceptance of the outside world as well as the choice of personality. As a matter of fact, there are various factors for the formation of values, including not only the influence from parents, seniority, teachers and peers in family, social and school life, but also the influence from individuals' accumulation of knowledge, cultural concept and ideological inspiration, as well as factors such as ideology, policy and mechanism in political, economic and legal areas. It is impossible that one's values are formed only under the influence of one factor, or the effect of just a few factors. In conclusion, there are a variety of factors influencing the formation of people's values, and it may be that one aspect of factors playing a major role and other factors playing a supporting role. But in any case, the influencing factors of values are by no means unique and isolated, but pluralistic and diverse.

We have motioned that values are a "yardstick" of value in people's mind, consciousness and the bottom of their hearts. They are stationed in people's life, words and deeds, and rooted inside people's mind and soul, which are the pivot supporting people's value cognition, value choice and value judgment. In fact, values constitute the center of the system of people's thought and action like a kernel of value. Around this center, values extend from the inside to the outside in line with different levels, like concentric circles, and on each level, values can find the vehicles for support and expression, and manifest themselves by dint of these vehicles. Therefore, the manifestations of values are also varied. For example, what style of clothes a person likes and what kind of taste he prefers are all related with his values. Meanwhile, the values of a person manifested at the level of food, clothing, housing, transportation and other basic necessities of life are different from the values represented by what kind of books he prefers and what style of music he appreciates. The former is the value pursuit at the level of material life, while the latter is related to another level, that is, the level of spiritual life.

As far as a social individual is concerned, his values are fully reflected in his thoughts, words and actions, in his ways of understanding and dealing with various matters, as well as in his daily practice; and as for a social group, its language, literature, art, philosophy of politics, customs, religion, lifestyle, institutional decisions and so on, are all able to express its intrinsic values. In order to facilitate understanding, people tend to classify the various concepts embodied in these objects into different areas, such as political concept, economic concept, cultural concept and social concept, but the core of all these concepts is always the values that guide people to make choices and decisions. As a matter of fact, values are an intrinsic standard of value that is deep rooted in the heart of an individual or a group and manifests itself through external objects. However some of these external objects only show the appearance of values and fail to truly represent the long-term, constant and typical values of a group. It is just because of this that in many cases, only through an in-depth exploration and careful differentiation, can people truly understand the values of a group.

## 2. The Manifestations of the Values of the Chinese

What kind of values Chinese people, especially the contemporary Chinese people have, is the theme that we try to illustrate in this book. As regards this theme, we will elaborate on it in the later chapters. But before this, we need to talk about in what forms the values of the Chinese are shown, that is, what are the manifestations of the values of the Chinese?

Once this question is raised, readers will feel it is a very difficult problem. Why? Because values is a quite complex system of value residing in people's minds, which is a generic term for people's thinking, cognition, value judgment and behavior guidance system. Values are closely combined with people and their minds, permeating in people's words, thoughts, behaviors and survival activities. In particular, people's life values are basically combined with their lives, thus they exist everywhere at any time, and may be manifested in any possible form, for this reason, it is difficult to enumerate them all. In view of this, we can only select some of the most important and typical manifestations to illustrate the existence and representation of the values of the Chinese.

### Ⅰ. Language & Words

As we all know, Chinese nation is a generic name for the fifty-six ethnic groups living in China at present, which is a complex ethnic integration. Since or even before a written history of China, the

Chinese specifically refers to those people living in Zhong Yuan (the Central Plains of China), generally referring to today's Henan and Southern Hebei Province. Those living in marginal areas and having different dialects, costumes and habits are regarded as barbarians or alien tribes. Later, after slow exchange and integration, Chinese people gradually formed a united nation, that is, the Chinese nation. Although they are all called the Chinese nation, those people who are derived from different origins and races brought different dialects, costumes, etiquette and custom, as well as habits of life and production. Actually, all of these embody their own cognition and judgment of value in the field of their life, production and survival, as well as their own values. Of course, these values are fragmentary and full of vitality, which would be gradually integrated and changed with the values of Zhong Yuan people in the later national integration and social interaction.

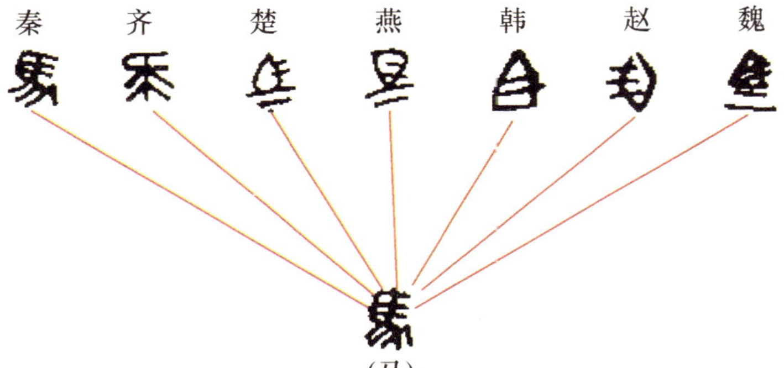

Unified Chinese characters under power of Qin

With the exchange and integration of all ethnic groups in the Chinese nation, the language was also unified. Prior to the Qin Dynasty, most vassal states have their own dialects and script. After Emperor Qin Shihuang (also called the First Emperor of China) unified the other six states, the Small Seal Script was adopted as the standard script, thus achieving the unification of the script. Later, also with the integration of ethnic groups, dialects in various areas were gradually merged, and slowly, a language that can reflect the common values of the Chinese took shape and was consolidated. Today, the common spoken language used by the Chinese people is Mandarin (Putonghua) and the script is commonly referred to as Chinese character. However, Mandarin and Chinese character are evolved and formed from the dialects and script over the long history, which contain contribution of all Chinese people of all ethnic groups as well as their ways of thinking, habits of life, and cognition of value, so we believe that the language reflects the ideological concept and the habit of being of the Chinese, and of course the values of the Chinese.

The language reflects the ideological concept and the habit of being of the Chinese, and of course the values of the Chinese.

Taking the two characters "国家" (country and home) as an example, their standard pronunciations in modern Chinese are "guo jia", the unification in terms of their pronunciation and type font expresses the unified cognition and judgment of the Chinese people, which originates from the meaning of the two characters contained in the ancient Chinese— "國" is the traditional form of "国", which, from the pictographic perspective, can be interpreted like this: "a soldier holding a halberd guards a territory with population and land", and "家": "A place where pigs live under roofs". From the interpretation of the character "国", people get to know that a country has its territory and population, and must be guarded by soldiers, thus they acquire a sense of identification with the land and population as well as a consciousness of safeguarding the boundaries of the country. From the interpretation of the character "家", people know that home means people and livestock coexist under the same roof, which brings people a sense of warmth, happiness and peacefulness. It is not only the ideological and cultural tradition of the Chinese people that passes on through the characters, but also the basic values about country and home that a Chinese people should have.

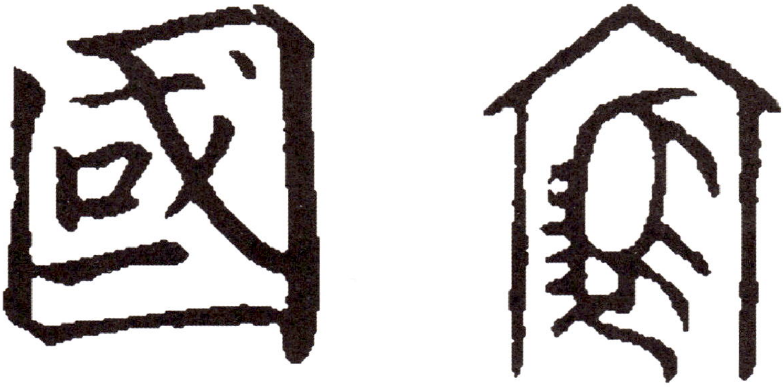

Evolution of Chinese characters "国" and "家"

Each Chinese character as well as its pronunciation is the component element of the Chinese culture, which also contains the values of the Chinese. How far-reaching the influence of the values contained by a unified language is depends on how widely it is spread. Today, many Chinese people, in particular minority groups continue using the languages created by their ancestors. Their languages, in themselves, are integral parts of the Chinese culture and Chinese civilization, and also contain the values of their own groups. This is the manifestation of the diversity and comprehensiveness of the Chinese culture, which is worth cherishing and protecting. At the same time, many minority groups that do not speak Chinese or write Chinese characters originally have learnt Mandarin and Chinese characters, and they have obtained benefits both economically and culturally in various ways from Han people that are in the majority, which greatly contribute to the progress and development of minority groups. By and large, Mandarin and Chinese characters that are widely used by the Chinese people contain their common values. Therefore, it is concluded that language is a basic form and an important vehicle that shows the values of the Chinese.

## Ⅱ. Food and Costumes

Not long before, a documentary television series *A Bite of China* which introduced Chinese food and culinary art aroused strong reactions both home and abroad. Many people who have watched this documentary are deeply touched by the culinary wisdom of the Chinese, fine food in China, as well as the living wisdom, life experience, perfect artistry and values behind Chinese food. Someone once said half-jokingly and half-seriously: if you are watching *A Bite of China* while having dinner, your appetite will be increased a lot; if you are watching *A Bite of China* not at dinner time, you will feel very hungry; if you are watching *A Bite of China* in your dream, you will taste all the delicacies over China; if you are watching *A Bite of China* while you are awake, you will feel happy about and proud of being a Chinese sincerely. You are happy because you are living in a country with such plentiful, beautiful and gorgeous culinary arts, and you are proud because you can feel that Chinese people are pursuing "beauty" while enjoying "food". The colorful and dazzling delicacies in China embody the emotions, thinking and values of the Chinese people over thousands of years. Indeed, at the time of singing the praises of the plentiful and beautiful Chinese food as well as the Chinese people's pursuit of the purest and most beautiful food, the documentary television series also make us reflect on the values of the Chinese in respect of food.

From the living realities of food and the food habits, which embody the wisdom of the Chinese, developed through thousands of years recorded in the documentary, as well as the pursuit of life and the living state reflected by these realities of food and food habits, we can easily find the values on survival, living and life in the bottom of the heart of the Chinese people. In *The Gift of the Nature*, we see that at the time of gaining food materials such as matsutake from Nature, Chinese people do not forget to protect the hyphae of matsutake, free young scallops, protect fish by increasing the mesh size, and grow young seedlings and sow new seeds, so as to continue the life of animals and plants. These good habits are undoubtedly the reflection of protecting the environment, paying back to nature and pursuing ecological civilization. In *The Story of Staple Food*, we learn various kinds of fondness for food all over China, Chinese people's ability and wisdom in gaining food materials according to local circumstances, and value pursuit with colorful local characteristics. In *The Inspiration of Transformation* and *The Taste of Time*, we realize the Chinese people's philosophy of food and rules for survival of being flexible, reasonable and patient. In *The Secrets of Kitchen* and *Flavors of the Harmonic*, we see the art of fire and water, the harmony between man and all Creation, the custom of filial piety and respect for elders expressed in the Chinese village feast, and the pursuit of harmony, persistence, tolerance, reunion, tranquility, smoothness and simplicity in food and life. In *Our Fields*, we comprehend the diligence, kindness, simplicity and honesty of the Chinese people in their pursuit of a beautiful life and appreciate their love and passion for life…

*A bite of China* (CNSPHOTO)

It is also the same case for costumes. In China, food is a kind of culture, so are costumes. There is Cheongsam, Tang suit and Chinese tunic suit; there is buttoned Chinese tunic, water sleeves and mandarin jacket; there is coarse cloth and silk, cotton fabric and jade clothes… In Chinese history, each dynasty has its own costume; in different regions of China, various ethnic groups also have their own costumes. The difference in food and costume is not only due to the geographical factors, but also related with the customs and cultural pursuit. For example, red clothes are often worn on wedding and festival days, because wearing red and decorating with colors means happiness and good fortune; while white

*The food and costumes of the Chinese contain their customs and cultural pursuit, as well as their values.*

clothes are often worn on memorial ceremcny and funeral, for wearing white and mourning implies misfortune and sadness, and so forth. Food and costumes embody the Chinese people's happiness, anger, grief and joy, represent their luck, position, longevity and festivity, and convey their perception, emotions, will and behaviors. In a word, the food and costumes of the Chinese contain their customs and cultural pursuit, as well as their values.

## Ⅲ. Architectural Landscape

Architecture is the humanized construction, which is both material and humanistic. This is not just a consensus reached by architects, but it seems that it has been a consensus of everyone in the society. In human society and the history of the world, there have been a variety of architectural systems, and each of them represents a different cultural pursuit and values. Chinese architecture, together with European architecture and Islamic architecture is called three major architectural systems in the world. Its long history, wide spread and glorious achievements make architecture enthusiasts so obsessed and also attract the interest of the travelers around the world, memorable to them. In the process of social development in China, there have been numerous magnificent architectural landscapes. Although some of them have collapsed with the ups and downs of the history, those that survive today are still worthy as the representatives of the Chinese styles and Chinese manners, for architectural landscape is also a reflection of the values of the Chinese.

The Chinese architecture, ranging from city walls, moats and palaces, Buddhist and Taoist temples, pagodas to folk houses and gardens, from the Great Wall that has lasted thousands of years and the north-south transcontinental Beijing-Hangzhou Grand Canal to today's Three Gorges Dam, from countless bridges and buildings to innumerable mausoleums and gardens, from timber construction, masonry construction to modern metal construction, and from upright column, cross beam to mesh structure and axis structure, all embodies the cognition, values, spirit and taste of the Chinese and portrays the institutions, etiquette, aesthetics and habits of the Chinese. In the final analysis, it is the values of the Chinese that are throughout various architectural landscapes.

Spectacular Earth Buildings in Fujian (CNSPHOTO)

City walls and moats are used for protection and defense, which not only reflect the enfeoffment system during the feudal era, but also represent the concept of the pursuit of peace and self-protection; palaces are the symbol of the dignity and solemnity of feudal imperial power, which imply a kind of inviolable supremacy; all landscapes, including the comfortable folk houses, extravagant gardens and placid Buddhist temples, contain the information of value. Taking folk houses for example, the tiled roof ridge in north China, the patio in south China, the screen wall in front of the house, the screen in the house, and the courtyard behind the house all have their distinctive characteristics and ingenious uses. Skylights are used for widening the vision and floor drains for draining. In addition to their own ingenious uses out of consideration for natural factors, people's feelings and moods play a larger part of the consideration. They may be used for privacy, for convenience, for comfort, and also for some kind of recognized standard of value. The quadrangle dwellings in Beijing not only take account of the order of family members, but also pay attention to the concord and convenience as well as the happiness and unity of a family. People living in the Loess Plateau in Northern Shaanxi Province acclimatize themselves to local conditions and use local materials to build cave dwellings on the hill slopes. These cave dwellings are warm in winter and cool in summer, low in construction cost, comfortable and beautiful, and have good sound insulation, which reflect the concept of harmony between man and nature. Besides, the earth buildings in Guangdong and Fujian provinces, the Mongolian yurts of Mongol ethnic minority, the stilted buildings of Tujia ethnic minority, the drum towers of Dong Village, the watchtowers of Qiang ethnic minority and the bamboo buildings of Dai ethnic minority are all the best choices made by the local people through combining the local realities with their own demands, especially their own value judgments. All these choices without exception embody their consideration for the value of nature, society, time and space, as well as human factors.

## Ⅳ. Philosophy and Art

The above description of the manifestations of the values of Chinese people is not inclusive, but just a small part of the countless vehicles for representing values. However, these manifestations, to a large extent, represent the survival value of the Chinese people in their daily lives and activities, as well as their value cognition and value choice. In addition to this, there are another kind of relatively abstract values, those are, cognitive values, which are largely manifested in philosophy, religion, literature, music, art, and other spiritual products of the Chinese. For example, Daoism represented by Laozi and Zhuangzi, Confucianism represented by Confucius and his descendants, Mohism represented by Mozi and other various doctrines and schools that originated in local China, as well as doctrines of Buddhism, Christianity and Islam that are introduced into China from foreign countries or areas, are all the ideological sources that construct this kind of abstract cognitive values. And the thinking mode and value cognition contained in them also profoundly influence and shape the values and spirit of the Chinese people. In short, the values contained in the traditional Chinese philosophy and religious culture are distinct and unique, which have a profound influence on the way of thinking and the way of act of the Chinese people.

> Chinese people have embedded rich information of value and conveyed plentiful concept of value in their literature and art.

Similar to the traditional philosophy, the innumerable traditional literature and art in China are also remarkable and splendid. From the ancient myth to the *Book of Odes* and the *Songs of Chu*, from the Music Bureau Poetry to folk songs of Northern and Southern Dynasties, from Tang Poetry, Song Ci, Yuan Drama to novels of the Ming and Qing Dynasties, essays of the

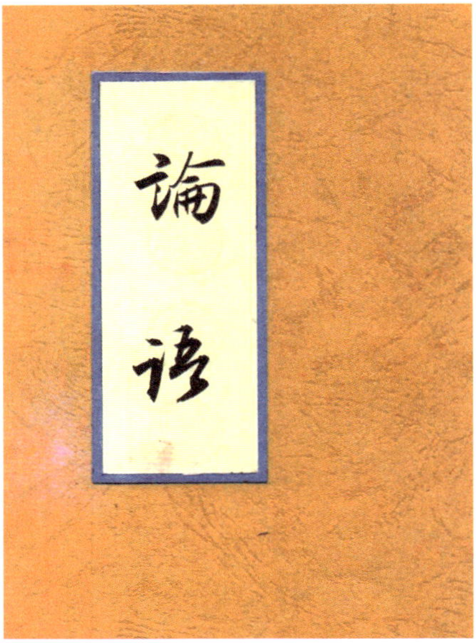

*The Analects* of Confucius

Republic of China, and to today's diverse literary and artistic forms, Chinese people have embedded rich information of value and conveyed plentiful concept of value in their literature and art. It is not exaggerated to say that each poem, each novel and each song contains some certain values in itself. For example, so many moods in the turbulent years are portrayed in the novel *Romance of the Three Kingdoms*; so many phenomena in the world of mortals are depicted in the novel *The Scholars*; so many cultural emotions are aroused by the song *Descendants of Dragon*, and so many feelings of nostalgia are evoked by the song *Nostalgia*.

The values of the Chinese people shown in philosophy, literature and art are the same as those shown in respect of food, clothing, architecture, medicine and festivals, which are all the reflections of the thinking and judgment of the value of some aspects in Chinese people's lives and production activities. Values are abstract and implicit, which are not easy to be described; but in another sense, values are distinctive and unique, if you pay careful attention to them, you will find they are right in your life and beside you, and finally will manifest themselves in the words and deeds of the Chinese people.

Apparently, only through the description from above few aspects, the values of the Chinese, as an enormous and complex research object, cannot be straightened out, nor can their connotations and meanings be fully expressed. Similar to all other nationalities' values in the world, the values of the Chinese are rooted in their life, production and survival. Therefore, in order to acquire in-depth understanding of the values of the Chinese, we must turn back to their life, their pursuit of survival and their production practice so as to analyze the primitive value choice made by the Chinese people.

## 3. The Western Evaluation of the Values of the Chinese

In the field of world civilization and cultural exchange, there is always a perspective of mutual observation and mutual evaluation. In the modern history of the thought exchange between China and the West, there are Chinese people opening their eyes to see the world, and there are also Westerners stretching out their necks to explore the Chinese mysteries. Over 10 years ago, some scholars compiled a series entitled *The West in the Eyes of China in 2000* and *China in the Eyes of the West in 2000*, which collects the images of China and the West left in the process of their imagining, feeling, knowing, understanding and getting familiar with each other in the 2000 years of history, showing both of their profound and superficial perspectives when Eastern and Western civilizations observe each other. The images of China that remain in the records of Western thinkers, theologians and travelers collected in the series, as well as those exquisite judgment and description of the Chinese people's words and deeds permeated between the lines, are exactly the portrayal of Chinese civilization and the values of China and Chinese people in the Westerners' evaluation system. Of course, such description and narration of them mostly are not direct, but obscure; thus, only through earnest and personal experience and observation can we realize them and only by meticulous exploration can we tell whether or not these records are accurate, pertinent, and proper.

## Ⅰ. The Sources of the Information about the Evaluation of the Values of the Chinese

Marco Polo

Since the 5th century B. C., the Westerners have had an initial impression on China. It was the light fabric called seres—silk that brought China into the cognitive world of Westerners. From then on, the East-West exchanges were begun slowly; besides the real life of the Chinese people, even their world of thought, spiritual pursuits and values began to gradually come into Westerners' sight and evaluation. After the Middle Ages, with the increased exchanges between China and Western countries, the image of the Chinese people, especially their values became clearer in the Westerners' minds, and relevant records also increased. Those well-known works such as *The Travels of Marco Polo*, *Book of the Estate of the Great Khan*, *The Decameron* and *Canterbury Tales* more or less record some landscapes, customs, characters and stories of China, through which we can roughly see the image of the Chinese people in the eyes of Westerners. There are a great many materials on this, so it is difficult to trace and mention them all. Thus, for the sake of accuracy, we only select some texts that describe the values of the Chinese people most directly to take a general view.

*The Travels of Marco Polo*, *Book of the Estate of the Great Khan*, *The Decameron* and *Canterbury Tales* more or less record some landscapes, customs, characters and stories of China, through which we can roughly see the image of the Chinese people in the eyes of Westerners.

In the 13th century, the merchant Marco Polo of Venice described the life and warfare of Tartars and their Monarch Genghis Khan in his travelogue, he said Tartars are hardworking, indomitable, brave, skilled in fighting, fearless of danger, and not afraid of difficulties and hardships, he also mentioned that they have their only God, morals and laws. Marco Polo also told about the details of the views, people, life and production in the cities in China, from which we can see the values of the local Chinese people. For example, when he recorded Hangzhou in his travelogue, he wrote:

> The residences of Hangzhou people are gorgeous and richly ornamented. They show great fondness for such ornament and painting as well as imaginative buildings, and this is very costly.[4]

He also added:

> Hangzhou local residents are peaceful in character. Their former monarchs were not warlike, and thus, under such influence, they develop a peaceful and elegant character. They know nothing about the use of weapons and never keep weapons in their houses. They run their business fairly and honestly. And people get along with each other and enjoy a friendly and harmonious relationship. ... Even those strangers who come here to do business are treated equally and sincerely. Local people may invite them to their homes at pleasure to express friendship and give kindly advice and help them in their commercial affairs.[5]

There are a lot of descriptions like this in the travelogue of Marco Polo, which all can reflect some sides of the values held by some people in some places in the traditional Chinese society. Of course, they were also the values of the Chinese.

Beginning with Marco Polo, a large quantity of travelogues, biographies and journals more or less record some values of the Chinese people. Among them the most worth mentioning are "the most affluent areas in the world" described by Odoric, Mandeville's *Travels of Sir John Mandeville*, Mendoza's *History of the Great and Mighty Kingdom of China and the Situation Thereof*, Matteo Ricci's *The Journals of Matteo Ricci*, the "Eastern Europe" called by Leibniz, the description of China by Voltaire in *Folklore*, as well as the description of the values of the Chinese people by Quesnay, Montesquieu, Macartney and Hegel in their academic or political writings.

In the late 19th century and early 20th century, a large number of American missionaries and scholars came to China and they carefully observed the values of the Chinese in their mission or teaching. Among the great many writings and literature left by them, some depict and portray the traditional Chinese people as well as their ideological concept and spiritual value at that time, which are worthy of our attention and can provoke contemporary Chinese people's deep thought.

Since the problem of values is a very large topic, which is reflected in all aspects of life, production and struggle practice of a society and its groups, it is indeed not easy to express the values of a society or a group in brief and extremely academic words. The descriptions of the values of the Chinese by those missionaries and scholars motioned above are not just a few insipid words, but have permeated through the details of the Chinese society and Chinese people observed and portrayed by them carefully. In view of this, it is difficult for us to summarize all their views on the values of the Chinese in simple words, and the best way is to find access to the information on this aspect.

In our opinion, such writings are directly related to the topic we are talking about here, which are: *Chinese Characteristics* by Arthur H. Smith, *Real Chinaman* by Holcombe Chester, *The Changing*

*Chinese* by E. A. Ross, *China*: *An Analysis* by Frank J. Goodnow and *The Lore of Cathay* by W. A. P. Martin, and so on.

From the early 20th century to the present, another century passed, during which there also emerge a lot of Western writings introducing and evaluating Chinese people. Among these writings, some have distinct political overtones and some are classic academic works; some cause ideological turmoil in the calm environment, and some reassure the people in the social unrest. The coming out of these writings also shows the Westerners' evaluation of the Chinese people, especially their values. American reporter Edgar Snow's *Red Star over China*, British author Han Suyin's *The Morning Deluge*, and John King Fairbank's *The Cambridge History of China* are all examples in point. Of course, these writings are not to specially describe the values of the Chinese, but only imply them in some respects, from some perspectives and to some extent.

## Ⅱ. The Evaluation Mixed with both Praise and Criticism

In general, Westerners have both favorable and unfavorable views on the values of the Chinese. Those holding a favorable view often highly praise the excellent Chinese civilization and the glorious Chinese culture, thus generating a feeling of yearning and admiration on the values of the Chinese. It should be said that such praise is not overrated, but generally is stating an objective fact. The Chinese nation has a long history of 5 000 years and has created the most admirable civilization and cultural achievements in human history, making an important contribution to human civilization. These achievements and contributions are the pride of the Chinese people. Throughout Chinese and foreign fields of thought, in this regard, all the people who have magnificent and broad view of history and know to regard human society, China and the Chinese civilization from the macro-historical perspective will agree. In fact, there are a lot of Westerners who praise Chinese civilization and Chinese history like Voltaire, Hegel and so on.

Of course, there are many Western observers who have little understanding of the Chinese civilization, culture and history, and they left their disdain for and criticism against China and Chinese people in their writings, among which, there is no lack of attack and criticism against the values of the Chinese. Regarding this situation, we need to mention that a lot of such kind of observers and thinkers observe or analyze the values of the Chinese under the influence of a strong ideological background, and they tend to comment China's political and social systems from their own political stance and value attitude, thus causing them to view the values of the Chinese with prejudice. Furthermore, some of them even simply make efforts to specially look for the deficiencies in character, thought, spirit and values of the Chinese people, and thereby defame the Chinese people by taking a part for the whole. However, after all, such situations are only a small minority.

A very interesting phenomenon is that almost all people who have observed China would mention the national character and values of the Chinese people, the only differences are that some of them mentioned it positively and some of them held an attitude of criticism, some mentioned it in more detail and some just talked about it briefly. Among those works concerning the evaluation of the values of the Chinese, *The Journals of Matteo Ricci* that once was the most influential work in the Chinese and foreign fields of culture and thought is a representative work. The author Matteo Ricci is an Italian missionary, who is also an important figure in the early history of Chinese and Western cultural exchanges. He had lived in China for 28 years, and he translated *Euclid's Elements*, and *Epitome Arithmeticae Practicae*, *Measurement Theory* etc. together with Chinese Ming Dynasty scientist and mathematician Xu Guangqi and Li Zhizao and wrote the memoirs of his life in China, that is, *China in the Sixteenth Century: The Journals of Matteo Ricci*, in his later years. In this book, Matteo Ricci praised that the Chinese people were the most industrious people, and most of them had strong mechanical process ability. He also considered that the Chinese people had business gifts and talents and were versatile. Moreover, in his view, the Chinese people are accustomed to living a frugal life and have an ingenuous temper. And in morality, the Chinese people attach the greatest importance to the five major virtues, viz. benevolence, righteousness, etiquette, wisdom and integrity, and emphasize to be considerate, respectful and polite towards others in handling matters. These are the depiction of the values of the Chinese from a positive side. But Matteo Ricci also thought that Chinese people were used to being arrogant because of their ignorance of the outside world, but once the truth was revealed, they would feel inferior. It should be admitted that Matteo Ricci's evaluation of the values of the traditional Chinese people is quite objective and fair, which includes both positive praise and negative comments.

The French Enlightenment thinker Montesquieu, who lived in the first half of the 18th century, conducted researches on the political system, institution, customs and etiquette of China in his great masterpiece *The Spirit of the Laws*. He discussed Chinese emperors'

Matteo Ricci

luxury and common people's diligence and frugality, researched into the values of population, land and labor of the Chinese people, and highlighted the qualities of their character, etiquette and morality. Besides, Montesquieu also mentioned the merits and defects in Chinese people's character, as well as the reasonable and biased aspects in their value judgment. He believed that Chinese religion, law, customs and etiquette were based on the combination of legislation and governance, while Chinese emperors' governance was on the basis of the thought of governing home and the life of Chinese people was totally under the guidance of etiquette. In order to maintain the life, the ordinary people could only choose to work hard, and subject to the needs of life or weather conditions, they had to be mercenary, but the law did not impose restrictions on this.

Similar to Montesquieu, another important French Enlightenment thinker Voltaire also made evaluation of and paid a lot of attention to Chinese culture and history, and he spoke more highly of the thought, culture, spirit and values of the Chinese people. He thought that the Chinese culture was not only much earlier and more civilized than Western culture, but also had the features of giving emphasis to tolerance, wisdom and harmony rather than superstition and fanaticism. He wrote:

> The vast and populous empire of the Chinese was governed like a family, while we were wandering in the forests of the Ardennes. ... Their religion was simple, wise, august, free from all superstition and all barbarity, ere we had yet Theutats.[6]

Voltaire clearly realized the wisdom and greatness of the Chinese, and he tried to avoid the prejudice due to ignorance while evaluating the Chinese people and Chinese society. One of his remarks may play a role of "rehabilitation" for Chinese civilization and society, and also play an "instructive" role for later generations' understanding of China, that is,

> The temerity we have shown, at the extremity of the west, of judging of this eastern court, and imputing atheism to them, has been vehemently attacked in an *Essay upon General History*. What, in fact, must have been the rage of some amongst us, to call an empire atheistical, when almost all its laws are founded upon the knowledge of a Supreme Being, Requiter, and Avenger?[7]

In order to understand the two views of evaluation more directly, we have listed several important thinkers' points of view so as to make a general view of the two entirely different views in the Western aca-

Voltaire

demic circles when they make comments on the values of the Chinese. It should be noted that these views mostly refer to the Chinese people in the traditional sense and seldom involve the values of the contemporary Chinese people after the reform and opening up. For historical reason, comparatively speaking, the comments of the Westerners on the traditional Chinese people as well as their values are much more than their evaluation of the values of the Chinese people in the current era. However, it is still not easy to just make evaluation of the traditional Chinese people and their values. China has an accumulation of civilization and culture of thousands of years, and it is ruled by the feudal ideology that is dominated by the Confucianism for over two thousand years. Confucianism has distinctive characteristics, which means it is able to create fairly consistent characteristics of personality and values. However, on the other hand, Chinese culture is undoubtedly too profound, even the system of Confucianism is a very complex system of values. The famous French thinker Jean-Paul Sartre once had a view on this. In 1955, Sartre visited China, and when he spoke about his impressions on the Chinese in an interview, he said:

> Confucianism has already become a system of etiquette, which, in a sense, is practiced by all the Chinese people every day. It is quite difficult to summarize a Chinese. This is not because he has anything to conceal from you, but it is precisely because that this system of etiquette requires him to keep cautious and self-restraint in interpersonal relationship, which however, is not the performance of resentment or indifference. [8]

> In the mutual observation between China and Western countries, what is more serious is not the mistakes in understanding that have been appeared or will appear again, or the fetters in exchanges brought by them, but rather the lack of an attitude of respecting each other and being willing to understand and accept each other.

Needless to say, even in the present cultural exchanges between China and the West, there will certainly be a lot of vague understanding or even misunderstanding about China and the values of the Chinese for one reason or another among Westerners, which will greatly hinder the cultural exchanges and social interaction at all levels between China and the West, and to some extent may also plant the seeds of alienation and resentment. A friendly, smooth and fruitful international exchange must be built on the basis that the two sides can understand each other, trust each other, and approach the ideological and cultural essence and intrinsic values of the other side as far as possible. Thus, in the mutual observation between China and Western countries, what is more serious is not the mistakes in understanding that have been appeared or will appear again, or the fetters in exchanges brought by them, but rather the lack of an attitude of respecting each other and being willing to understand and accept each other. The purpose of this book is exactly to introduce an objective and real system of thought and values of the Chinese to the outside world, which, in a certain sense, is intended to make contributions to the exchanges and intercourse between China and the West.

## 4. New Changes in the Values of the Contemporary Chinese

The values of the contemporary Chinese have undergone great changes compared with the historical and traditional ones. The reasons for the changes in the values of the Chinese, fundamentally speaking, are the social change and opening up in China as well as the changes in production and life of the Chinese society. Since 1978, the Chinese society has undergone an earth-shaking change, that is, the "reform and opening up" which is quite familiar to the Chinese people. The reform is an overall and comprehensive change with unprecedented depth and breadth, which enables China to get rid of the shackles of the old relations of production and the rigid way of thinking and make great steps towards modernization. The opening up is a wide and multi-level opening with unprecedented horizons and ambition, which enables China and the Chinese people to embrace the world with a broad perspective, open-minded spirit and confident state of mind and begin to integrate themselves into the process of globalization.

> The reform and opening up changes the way of thinking, ideological concept and value orientation of people.

The reform and opening up causes significant changes in the social production, social structure and social relations in China, makes the economic component, mode of organization, way of employment, interest relationship and mode of distribution in the society become increasingly diversified, and also changes the way of thinking, ideological concept and value orientation of people. A lot of past ideological forbidden zones are broken; some impossible things become possible; and a number of unacceptable behaviors begin to be tolerated and accepted by people. In the reform and changes of the society, the values of the contemporary Chinese have appeared new trends and shown new characteristics in some areas. So, what are these new trends and new characteristics?

First, the values become diversified and complex. Diversification means that the values have possessed diverse ideological foundations, while complexity means that the values become more varied and also more difficult to grasp. After the reform and opening up, China has opened itself to the outside world more considerably, the Western lifestyle, social thought, doctrines and values have been pouring into China. Different behavioral principles, ideologies and belief systems generate a feeling of freshness in the Chinese people and allure them, coupled with the weakening influence of Chinese Confucianism in the contemporary era; therefore, many Chinese people have accepted the values that are based on the foreign culture and ideological foundation, which makes the values of the contemporary Chinese present a situation of diversification and complexity. For example, from the founding of the People's Republic of China to the reform and opening up, Chinese people believed in the social values of collectivism; however, after the reform and opening up, with the penetration of Western individualistic thinking, many of the Chinese in modem times stress the individual subject consciousness and put emphasis on the importance of and respect for individual interests. In this case, although the values of collectivism are still the mainstream, they are facing an unprecedented challenge.

Second, the conflicts and struggles over values are increasing. Such a trend is linked with the diversification and complexity of the values of the contemporary Chinese. In the past, most people had a common ideological foundation of values and also believed in a generally consistent law of values, thus under the guidance and control of the dominant values of the society, there were less contradictions and conflicts of values between people. However, it is not the same case today. the more and more diverse and varied values not only bring about contradictions to individuals in their minds and behaviors, but also create conflicts over the value choice of different people. Regarding the same thing or same phenomenon, the past relatively consistent standard of value judgment will no longer take effect or can only play an obviously weakening role, whereas the Self values that highlight personality and individual subjectivity have become the law dominating people's value choice. Hence the contradictions and conflicts of values between people increase, and in some areas, some aspects, there even appear serious struggles over values.

Third, the world of value becomes illusory and disorderly. The world of value is a special spiritual world, which always needs stable standards and constant laws. If the laws of value that play a unifying and guiding role are lost, the world of values of people will become disorderly, which may also easily lead to the losing of values. It's true that the diversified and complex values, to a certain extent, can free people's minds and inject spiritual vitality to the society and individuals, but meanwhile their negative effects cannot be underestimated, that is, they will make people's world of value become illusory and disorderly. Since the reform and opening up, many Chinese people become rich and generous in material, but in spirit and values, they feel nothing but lost and confused, they are powerless in the face of value choices and at a loss while making behavioral choices, which are exactly the manifestations of the illusory and disorderly world of value.

Of course, the changes in values brought about by the reform and opening up are not always negative, and they are also able to exert positive effects in many ways. For example, they can inspire people's thoughts, promote their exchange of ideas and activate their thinking as we have mentioned above. As is known to all, ideology is dominated by the values and it is the manifestation of values. Since the reform and opening up, Chinese people have gradually improved their awareness of opening, independence, competition, efficiency, fairness, contract, democracy, law, innovation and so on, which embody the changes in people's values. And the transformation of ideologies brought by such changes is beneficial to the construction of a modern country, a modern society as well as a modern individual personality.

## Notes

[1] *Encyclopedia of China • Psychology*, Beijing: Encyclopedia of China Publishing House, 1998, p. 154.

[2] *Encyclopedia of China • Sociology*, Beijing: Encyclopedia of China Publishing House, 1998, p. 113.

[3] Stephen Robbins, *Organizational Behavior* (7th Edition), Beijing: China Renmin University Press, 1997, p. 138.

[4] [5] *The Travels of Marco Polo*, Fuzhou: Fujian Science and Technology Publishing House, 1981, p. 179.

[6] Voltaire, *Essai Sur les Moeurs*, Volume one, Beijing: The Commercial Press, 1994, p. 87.

[7] Voltaire, *The Philosophy of History*, New York: Philosophical Library, 1965, p. 87.

[8] Cited from "Views on the New China", The journalist of *The New Statesman and Nation* K. S. Karol's interview with Sartre, in *The New Statesman and Nation*, Dec. 3, 1955, p. 737.

## Chapter Two

# The Endless Survival Values

# 2 The Endless Survival Values

Survival is the fundamental value of life, which is a matter of importance for a nation. Throughout the ages, there's no national community that thinks little of the survival problem, and there's no country that can ignore the survival problem of its nationals. Fundamentally speaking, the existence and development of human beings, in essence, is a problem about why and how they survive, in other words, whether or not human beings can survive and in what ways they survive. Therefore, the problem of survival becomes the important values, and it is the fundamental problem for measuring the significance and ways of the existence of people or a community.

> Life is what I desire, and so is righteousness. If I cannot have them both, I would rather choose the latter and forsake the former.

Chinese people think much of life and make more account of its value, but regarding the problem of life and survival, they have their own dialectic on them. In the dialectic between living and existing or life and death, we can see the distinctive survival values of the Chinese. In the value system of Chinese culture and the depths of the hearts of Chinese people, "living" and "existing" are two very important concepts, and they are closely connected with each other, constituting the kernel that dominates the Chinese people's understanding of the problem of life. "Living" means to create and continue life, while "existing" means to maintain the existence of life. The Chinese cultural system takes the care of life as its highest purpose and regards the existence and development of human life and even the state of life as the ultimate goal that people pursue. Thus, in the values of the Chinese, the deference and obedience to human life is quite prominent, man as well as the value of his life is the be-all and end-all of the Chinese and Chinese culture. Survival is material, while the value of survival and life is spiritual. Mencius said: "Life is what I desire, and so is righteousness. If I cannot have them both, I would rather choose the latter and forsake the former. "[1] From this saying, we can learn about Chinese people's expectation of the life and the value of life, as well as the principle of making choices between life and righteousness.

## 1. The Traditional View of Fate of the Chinese

Until today, among those proverbs that have been long popular, one proverb— "human life is predestined" is still familiar to quite a lot of Chinese people. When a person suffers some hardship, he may murmur these words in deep remorse; or, when he meets something happy, he may also utter these words complacently. This proverb reflects the traditional Chinese people's view of fate in their minds. One of the foundations of such view of fate is Confucius' "theory on the universe". In brief, the view of fate believes that man's life and fate are not in the hands of themselves, instead, it is the Heaven somewhere that controls man's life, longevity and fortune. In the traditional sense, the view of life of the Chinese is exactly a kind of view of fate, which is a thinking mode and a basic concept that link human life with the fate.

Qu Yuan, who is a great Chinese poet in the Pre-Qin Period, in his *Heavenly Questions* proposed simple scientific questions: "Who passed down the tales in the beginning of creation? … Yin and Yang are mixed together, but which of them is the origin? The sky has nine layers, but who manages and measures it?" As a matter of fact, they are asking how the heaven and earth were created and how the universe was formed. It seems that there have been scientific answers to these questions today, but at that time, such questions were beyond doubt extremely difficult for our ancestors. For only relying on the limited knowledge of nature, self and society acquired by them, these questions were rather hard to be answered. Thus, along with these questions, a lot of mythical tales, like the myth of Pan Gu who were said to have created the world by separating the heaven and the earth, the myth of Nüwa who created mankind with earth, the myth of Jingwei who was a mythical bird trying to fill the ocean with stones and so on, began to emerge, spread and take root in the ideological world of the Chinese. Whether they come from imagination or there indeed are some legendary records, in the eyes of the Chinese in the ancient times, these miraculous and great characters are gods with supernatural power, who are the incarnation and manifestation of the power of Heaven. They are the representatives of Heaven but also linked with mankind, which is a natural choice in the minds of ancient people. Ancient people do not possess the mighty power like them, but they need to link the power with themselves, so that they can find confidence and foundation for their own existence. Therefore, in the minds of ancient people, Heaven and man are integrated together.

Human power comes from nature, and human life comes from Heaven; the formation of such concept initially is because human beings realized the mightiness of natural power and the tininess of human power in their struggle with Nature. In many cases, due to the low technological level and cognitive ability, human beings can only

Qu Yuan

obtain life resources from nature; thus, human life, to a great extent, is conditioned by nature, and even depends on its gift and endowment. However, Nature, as Heaven, is not far away from man, which can not only provide resources and nourishment for human survival, but also bestow favors on man as he wishes. On the basis of abiding by Heavenly rules, Heaven and man are integrated, and thus, the world view of "harmony between man and Heaven" becomes the philosophy of ancient Chinese people, and the way of survival under the guidance of such philosophy shapes the traditional view of fate of the Chinese.

In such a view of fate, there are conflicts between man and Heaven, thus, they will not always be totally in accordance with each other, however, nor will they be totally separated from each other, and ultimately, they will be integrated and united together.

> Man is the most highly endowed among all creatures. Heaven sees and hears what man sees and hears.

Therefore, different from the mode of thinking in Western religion or creation myth that man should absolutely submit to some deity or god, in the conception of ancient Chinese people, man and Heaven are united, perhaps man cannot escape his fate, but human power still can conquer nature, as the ancient saying goes: "man can conquer nature". In the *Book of History • Great Speech*, it says "man is the most highly endowed among all creatures. Heaven sees and hears what man sees and hears", which implies the affirmation of the subject status and subject role of man.

In the traditional view of fate, what takes first place is man's worship of Heaven. In ancient Chinese people's understanding, nature is divided into three realms: heaven, mortal world and hell. People believe that outside the real natural world they are living, there is a heaven where the paramount ruler Jade Emperor and his concubines as well as countless divine troops live, and only those moral and talented people in the mortal world, where most people are common mortals who live mortal lives, can ascend to heaven and become immortals; whereas all those ordinary people will die, and those perpetrators will be thrown into hell to be punished. In the conception of the Chinese, heaven is good and beautiful, and the mortal world is ordinary, while hell is ugly and frightening. People in the mortal world will always get old on day. If a person is able to ascend to heaven, it means that he has entered into the kingdom of happiness and gotten rid of all miseries; whereas those who are thrown into hell will either turn into beasts of burden and continue to suffer punishment in the next life, or will never be freed and get new life. The gradually better realms from hell to the mortal world and then to heaven provide people living in the secular world with an active life impetus to strive to ascend to heaven and avoid being cast into hell. In order to achieve this purpose, people in the mortal world should comply with the rules of morality and etiquette, that is to say, they should keep striving to get opportunities of being good and avoid evil consequences.

Those who develop rules of morality and etiquette are the ones holding the power of law enforcement on behalf of Heaven, whose supreme ruler is the spokesman of Heaven, that is, the "Son of Heaven". In ancient China, only the emperor can be called the Son of Heaven, for only he is the son of Heaven, the legitimate representative of Heaven, and the one who is sent to the mortal world by Heaven to rule and manage this world. In order to express his identity as the Son of Heaven as well as his gratitude to Heaven for its grace, the emperor should conduct grand ceremonies of Sacrifice to Heaven. Standing in awe of the Mandate of Heaven, people are bound to obey the will of Heaven and submit to the rule of the emperor. Making use of such logic and mythical authority, the emperor becomes a secularized ruler in the view of fate of the Chinese. Although the emperor is still a human being, he is by no means an ordinary one, but the one grasping the absolute power over life and death. In the feudal society of China that lasted for over two thousand years, the emperor was the supreme authority that determined the lives and rights to live of the mortals. During the over two thousand years, for the sake of divine and secular power, the emperor, under the authority and glory of Heaven, governed the thoughts of the Chinese and also formally controlled the view of life of the Chinese.

Temple of Heaven

Then, how do ordinary people view such kind of life that is granted by Heaven? In the eyes of many Chinese people, birth and life are two different things: being born means good fortunate, and having life means happiness. Man's birth is out of chance, which is a Heaven-sent opportunity; man's life is also a gift of Heaven, but it does not exclude man's efforts after the birth. In other words, one's struggle and hard work in the world can only exchange for the chances of changing his fate; as for the things that he can or cannot obtain in the next life, it is impossible for him to make any change by means of his subjective will. Man's struggle and hard work can only lead to the changes in his life after birth. However, in the traditional view of fate, even one's life after birth, whether it is changeable or unchangeable, has been predestined and already arranged by Heaven; man just lives his life in accordance with the arrangement of Heaven. It is readily seen that in the traditional view of fate of the Chinese, fatalism is a dominant concept. Since such fatalism is beneficial to the so-called feudal rule arranged by Heaven, it is highly welcomed by the rulers. Over the past two thousand years, such a view of fate has still remained in the minds of some Chinese people, although it is no longer the dominant values nowadays, it has not completely disappeared as yet.

In Chinese society, there is still an informal profession—fortune-telling, which has a long history in China. Once it was quite popular in some eras. Of course, in Western society, there also appeared prophets like palm reader or fortune teller at one time. However, different from Western prophets who place emphasis on the prophecy of future, Chinese fortune-tellers not only predict and foretell the future, but also tell about the previous life of man, and often link up the previous life, this life and next life together to predict the transition of man's fate based on a standard or values. For example, a fortune teller may tell you that in your previous life, you were Wenquxing (a God of Literature and Art) in heaven, the one who is wise and talented. You are the reincarnation of Wenquxing, therefore you are more intelligent and more possible to achieve success in literature and art as well as other areas that are closely related to talent and intelligence. And then, he will tell you that you will be a man of letters with outstanding literary or artistic talent in the coming days. This fate is Heaven-sent and predestined. Such a fatalistic prophecy may be rooted in the lives of some people, and imperceptibly but inexorably becomes dependable values that support human life and survival, and thereby turns into an excuse of those people who believe in this fate for either striving for better results or making no more effort and simply waiting for the "pie in the sky".

Since long time ago, the ancient Chinese have cried "man can conquer nature", and along with the flourishing of science and the improvement of human ability and technology to transform nature, atheism also appeared and began to be known to more and more people; however, the belief in "life is fated, so are riches and honor" has always been like a continuous chain intertwined in the minds of the Chinese people, forming their view of life. Well, why do the Chinese value "fate"? For this, there are two reasons:

First, the formation of the view of fate is related to the process of man's transformation of nature and the fight against Heaven. Generally speaking, when the power of man is inferior to that of Heaven, people will realize that there is an irresistible power beyond their own ability that they cannot manage and control, thus, they tend to be resigned to fate. Heaven and fate provide people with a sense of dependence, which makes people become numb in soul and also feel hopeful in submission. Just as the example mentioned above, even if a person clearly knows that he is not some reincarnation of Wenquxing, he is still willing to believe such a lie of the fortune-teller, so that he can find a sense of superiority in it.

Second, for an organized society, the view of fate is conducive to its stability and order. The supreme authority of Heaven and fate as well as their paramount controlling force make the ordinary people feel afraid and in awe, and thus restrict their thinking and behavior. As a result, there will be more obedience and less disobedience, more consistency and less difference.

In traditional Chinese view of fate, people believe that there is a kind of power of Heaven beyond human power, and people are subject to the constraint of the Mandate of Heaven that they cannot control, nevertheless, in the face of their own fate, they may not necessarily be totally powerless. In fact, many people will regard the Mandate of Heaven as some sort of constant law or the "principle" of life after acquiring fairly scientific understanding of nature and external power. Facing this constant law, people don't always have to wait passively, but can adapt to it actively, for which there are two reasons: one is to prolong life, and the other is to make their lives more valuable and significant. Therefore, those who pursue high value of life will carry forward the "principle" of life and put it in the first place. For them, life is precious, but moral principles are more valuable and should be cherished. In a certain sense, the traditional view of fate reflects a kind of culture, which is a way of interpreting the relationship between man and nature, and it also reflects the way of thinking and value judgment of the ancient Chinese people. In such a way of thinking and value judgment, there contains the Chinese people's interpretation and positioning of the understanding of life.

> One of the core values throughout the traditional Chinese view of fate is "life".

One of the core values throughout the traditional Chinese view of fate is "life", i. e. the endless life, which refers to the emergence, growth and the continuation of life of all creatures. Chinese people respect and value the concept of "life" very much, and there have been doctrines and evaluation in this regard since long time ago. As the old saying goes "production and reproduction is what is called change", "the greatest attribute of heaven and earth is the giving and maintaining of life", the purport it expresses is that a general rule of the boundless universe is the endless life and the constant changes; the life, living and survival of man are no exception. With the aim of survival and reproduction, both the material life and spiritual life of man should be prolonged. However, all the efforts for the sake of the prolongation of man's material life will fall through along with death at last, whereas the efforts for the sake of the prolongation of man's spiritual life can be immortal owing to the "great virtue, great conduct and great learning".

In traditional Chinese society, people know the mandate of Heaven and stand in awe of it, but meanwhile they have no fear of fate; people have no means to prolong their natural life-span, but they can extend their spiritual life by means of the pursuit of the value of life. It should be admitted that this is indeed a wise way that the ancient Chinese people find to resolve the contradiction between life and fate, which reflects the living wisdom of the Chinese. Today, it seems that there may be nothing strange about the view of fate of the Chinese; however, at the turn of the 20th century, when it was introduced into foreign countries and cultures by the missionaries and thinkers who came to China, it was often classified as ridiculous, pitiful and even ignorant view of life, which seemed to be not worthy of appreciation and difficult to win acceptance and respect. If we take a look at the writings that introduce the Chinese people's view of life by many missionaries, we can find that such an attitude is rather obvious. It should be noted that the traditional view of fate of the Chinese is linked with Chinese creation myths, just like the relationship between the view of fate of the Westerner and Western religious and mythology of genesis. They both reflect a kind of value judgment of life at the time of the genesis of Chinese and Western cultures, which may not be fully acceptable at the present time, but their emergence is of inevitability at that time.

## 2. The Modern View of Life of the Chinese

The modern time is an economically developed, socially progressive and scientifically prosperous era. Although the influence of the view of fate that spread in ancient times has not completely disappeared in modern society, the Chinese people in modern times have gotten rid of the ideological ignorance caused by poor science and backward technology, and they no long fully uphold the traditional view of fate, but have a modern view of life and hold the modern understanding of man and life. Of course, the traditional view of fate and the modern view of life are not diametrically opposed to each other; there are both differences and certain connection between them.

In the ideology of the Chinese nation and the spiritual world of the Chinese people, valuing life is an important and prominent concept, and its fundamental aim is to wish that life can be long or constantly continued. However, the continuation of life is always in need of some conditions and confronted with challenges. Under what circumstances will people suffer misfortunes, and why do people give up their lives? When Mencius spoke of "forsaking life for righteousness", he still had some other works that contain the values of life, and as a matter of fact, in the traditional Chinese society, it is such values of life that dominate people's value choice of life and living. Up to today, the inner soul of such values is still unchanged, and perhaps this is one of the connections between the traditional view of fate and the modern view of life of the Chinese. In order to see this connection more clearly, we might as well excerpt these words as follows:

> To be sure, life is desirable, but I will not stick to it discreditably if something more precious is to be desired. I hate death, but I will not shun it when there is something more abhorrent than it. To make life one's greatest desire, what would one not resort to if only he could preserve it? To make death one's greatest abhorrence, what would one not do if only he could avert it? Hence there is something not to be resorted to even for the preservation of life and something not to be done even for the evasion of death. Therefore, that one would prefer righteousness to life and abhor iniquity more than death is not only the case with sages, but is also true of everybody. [2]

From these words, we can see that both life and death are a kind of value, which however, may be not the highest value that people think much of. If they are the highest value, then in order to achieve this value, one can give up everything else; while if they are not the highest value, then to give them up becomes possible. In Mencius' view, there is the value that is more important than life and death, that is, "righteousness". In traditional Chinese society, the feudal rulers set various sorts of virtues, such as benevolence, righteousness, etiquette, wisdom and integrity, which are also more important than life and death in terms of the value. These virtues have become the intrinsic value beyond man's life and death, as well as a tool of social indoctrination. As Mencius said, the sage and the wise may go after profits and avoid disadvantages and pursue the highest value of life, so do the common people. People in ancient times could give no thought to their own life and death for the sake of some righteousness, or use all means for their life and death; well, in this regard, isn't it the same case for the people living today?

Menci

At the beginning of this chapter, we have already mentioned that the understanding of life reflects the primary values of a nation or a group and embodies this nation or this group's first judgment about its survival value. Also, we have just discussed the view of fate of the Chinese in the traditional society. Such a view of fate believes that in man's life, there is a kind of transcendental value outside the value in himself, which is not controlled and realized by man himself, but fated by Heaven. A lot of foreigners in early period who observed Chinese society and culture once evaluated the religion and superstition in China, and many of Westerners believe that the thinking structure and the state of mind of the Chinese nation seem to be imbued with the concept of superstition. It seems that the traditional view of fate is just the case in point. But what's more important is that superstition is not the true spiritual pursuit of the Chinese people; although many of them still have believed in fate even until today, such belief in fate does not necessarily result in the hundred-percent conviction and absolutely pure religiosity.

Chinese people believe that there is a God, but the god in your mind and the god in mine are not always the same one. From the religious perspective, traditional Chinese people are pantheists and polytheists. Since it is the case, there will not be a unified god that constitutes a religion as a whole in China just like the religion in the Western society. Thus there will never be a unified value of religion throughout the process of the lives of the Chinese; even as regards fate, it is still the same case. If their lives are fated to be beautiful and happy, all the Chinese will accept with pleasure. However, if their lives are doomed to be miserable and disastrous, the modern people will not be resigned to their fate like the people in traditional society. In modern society, many people do not that easily resign themselves to adversity and reconcile themselves to visitation. At this time, the idea that man can conquer nature might prevail. In the face of misfortune and adversity, the modern Chinese people do not take them lying down, instead, they want to resist and struggle, and redeem and emancipate themselves from fate. This is also the performance of losing the worship of "Heaven" in the view of life of the modern Chinese people as well as its difference from the view of fate of the traditional Chinese people.

The idea of seeking redemption and emancipation from the miserable fate is prevalent in the traditional Chinese people, but less prevalent in modern people. Chinese people have always cherished their lives since the ancient times. As a folk proverb goes, "it would be better to live a poor life than die with dignity", this proverb is enough to show that Chinese people treasure their survival and lives a lot. Of course, their survival and lives are always for some purpose, or in other words, people exist for realizing some kind of significance. Such purpose or significance may be some external material goal or some internal spiritual needs. In the Chinese cultural tradition, the only value to which it is worthy to sacrifice man's life is "righteousness". Therefore, in the ideological tradition of the Chinese people, "forsaking life for righteousness" is a value choice that has existed since ancient times. However, only in some sort of man-made system of indoctrination for certain purposes, there emerges a doctrine of another dimension, that is, life is not precious enough, or to live is no better than to die.

In fact, the first principle of cherishing life is never to give up life so easily, which means one should not choose to die as long as there is hope and chance of life. Death means destruction, and a simple expression of actively choosing to die is "self-destruction". In the discourse system and ideology of Chinese people, self-destruction is undesirable, or even is a kind of taboo in life. If a person always has good luck and lives in favorable circumstances since he was born, then everything is satisfied; whereas if he only has bad luck and lives in adverse circumstances, then what he should do is to not give up, but to fight, for fight means to redeem and emancipate himself from fate. At this moment, the most power-

In the discourse system and ideology of Chinese people, self-destruction is undesirable, or even is a kind of taboo in life.

ful doctrine that Chinese people believe in is "nature can conquer man, but man can also conquer nature".

Of course, compared to the traditional view of fate of the Chinese people in ancient times, the modern view of life of the Chinese people has also undergone great changes. The most fundamental cause for the changes in the view of life of the Chinese still lies in the changes in their philosophy of life. Each era has its own philosophy of life, and people under the influence of different eras will hold different survival purposes and development goals, thus there will be different judgment of the meaning and value of life. Philosopher Zhang Junmai once paid a lot of attention to the problem of the philosophy of life. He said, there might be differences of opinion over the same life owing to different points of observation, therefore, the greatest disunity in the world at all times was the philosophy of life. The development and continuation of life is subject to the influence of external environment, and people's views on life are also various due to both internal and external factors. Obviously, the differences between traditional society and modern society, the living conditions of people, and their judgment of the meaning of life all bring about different changes in the modern Chinese people's understanding of life.

For modern Chinese people, life has been different from the fate in the traditional society; of course, the gift of life is the combination of chances and inevitability, but it has no longer been attributed only to Heaven. Under the interpretation and proof of modern science and technology, the past concept of regarding life as a gift from Heaven has returned to its natural, physiological and social nature. Life is no longer the gift of Heaven, but a right of all living things themselves.

Meanwhile, once people get their lives, they not only win the right to live, but also assume the obligation of life at the same time. Since that is the case, then in the ideological concept of modern people, life is not just a right to live, but also an obligation to live, that is to say, it is a unity of right and obligation, and it is just because of this that life means both enjoyment and responsibility. In the conception of modern Chinese people, the life of an individual is no longer owned by Heaven, or controlled by the monarch as in the past. The past situation that "life and death is in the hands of the monarch" has gone forever, the right to life of modern people must be respected and upheld. The life of an individual not only requires self-respect, but also needs to win the respect of the society and others. Thus, man's life and survival not only have dignity, but also obtain freedom.

For modern Chinese people, life is still a process of living, but it is independent, free and with dignity.

For modern Chinese people, life is still a process of living, but it is independent, free and with dignity. The process of living is a process of enjoying the right of life and fulfilling the obligation of life as well, which contains both demand and contribution. Demand means that people should gain the material rewards and spiritual encouragement and honor that they deserve, as well as the dignity and respect that they win from the society and others; contribution means that people should also equally offer something to others and the society within their powers in return for their respect and favors, in which there are both material and spiritual contribution.

Unlike the ancient Chinese people who believe in the traditional view of fate, modern Chinese people has gotten rid of the superstition of heaven and earth and begin to examine the process of life and survival with rational thinking, believing that they themselves are the masters who create and enrich their lives. The old concept of pinning their hopes on the afterlife has become less important, or even no longer been their hopes of life. What people value are the reality and the living process of life. The creation of life is no longer for the purpose of making the afterlife more brilliant, ascending to heaven, or winning wealth and rank in the next life, but for the richness and splendor of this life. It should be admitted that the modern Chinese people still cannot completely get rid of the problem of questioning the meaning of life. However, their understanding of the origin and process of life has been different from the past, therefore they will become more realistic, pay more attention to the earthly feelings and experiences, and be more adept at discovering the beauties in this world.

Compared to the traditional view of fate, the value choice in the life of modern people becomes freer, more diverse and more flexible. People's choice of the ways of realizing their lives is also effectively protected by the society. Meanwhile, the government and society's respect for and protection of people's right to life are increasingly strengthened. In the right to life, people's right to live and right to develop occupy the dominant position, and the improvement of people's living conditions and status is the basis of their right to live and right to develop. Since the reform and opening up, China has made remarkable achievements in its economic growth, over one billion people have broken out of poverty, and people's standard of living and quality of life are gradually improved. This is the most direct and practical manifestations of the respect for and the development of

*The National Human Rights Action Plan (2009—2010) Evaluation Report*

man's right to life. In June 2012, the Chinese government released the National Human Rights Action Plan (2012—2015), which is the second national action plan with the special theme of the development of human rights. This Plan caters to all Chinese people's new expectation of better life, and will continue to give top priority to the protection of people's right to live and right to develop so as to effectively improve the protection of people's economic, social and cultural rights. It can be said that the changes in the view of life of the modern Chinese people not only affect and demand the promotion of the life protection project, but also are inseparable from its implementation and support. It is just because of the social, policy and institutional protection that the will of life and the consciousness of survival of the Chinese people have been unprecedentedly improved.

## 3. The Survival Values of the Chinese

> The objects involved in the survival values are much richer than that in the view of life, and meanwhile the contents contained in them are also much more complex.

In brief, the survival values are the fundamental views of life and development. The starting point of survival values is the thinking on the questions about how human life is obtained, what rules of life should be followed, and so on. As we all know, birth and death are the two points in the cycle of life: birth means the beginning of life, the process of the development of life is exactly the process of the existence of life; death means the end of life, for atheists, death means the end of everything, as the saying goes "as we know, everything is empty after death". However, for theists or religious people, death perhaps means rebirth, or the beginning of a new life cycle. In such religious cognition, birth means beginning, but death does not necessarily mean the end. Therefore, in terms of the survival values, the first problem needs to be handled is how a nation, a group or a community look upon, measure and evaluate the life of man, for the value choice is contained in the process of life. But, the view of life belongs to one kind of survival values, which is the fundamental view of the problem of life. Life is a prerequisite for survival, only there is life, the problem of survival can be discussed; however, obtaining a life is not the entire content of survival. After a man is born, he just has the first condition of survival, and there will be a lot of objects, matters and categories that may produce specific values in the process of his life after birth, and all these values can be collectively referred to as survival values. Comparatively speaking, the objects involved in the survival values are much richer than that in the view of life, and meanwhile the contents contained in them are also much more complex.

If a nation, a county or a social group wants to survive and develop for long, it must own a set of values that play a dominant role. This perhaps is one of the most important revelations that the history of human development and progress can give us. Different countries, different nations may believe in different ideological value systems in different times, but such an ideological value system is indispensable, regardless of its contents, manifestations or whether it can successfully take root in people's minds and belief systems. It is not only related to the stability, unity and unification of a county, a nation or a society, but also can affect the order of the times and the change of civilization. French thinker Gustave Le Bon has some enlightening words that are enough to support our view here. He said:

> The great upheavals which precede changes of civilizations, such as the fall of the Roman Empire and the foundation of the Arabian Empire, seem at first sight determined more especially by political transformations, foreign invasion, or the overthrow of dynasties. But a more attentive study of these events shows that behind their apparent causes the real cause is a profound modification in the ideas of the peoples. The true historical upheavals are not those which astonish us by their grandeur and violence. The only important changes whence the renewal of civilizations results, affect ideas, conceptions, and beliefs.[3]

There are a lot of external factors that can cause changes in people's ideas, conceptions, and beliefs, however only their values system is changed, or in other words, their survival values are radically changed, can a significant change become possible.

The civilization of Western society has gone through thousands of years of development, during which, there certainly are social transformations and continuous generation of new ideas and concepts. It is the revolution led by the bourgeoisie and the society created by them that replace the long-term feudal rule. Since the Age of Enlightenment in Europe, people's concepts especially the system of values have been gradually changed. The ideas of liberty, equality and fraternity proposed in the French Revolution have become the banner of values leading to the victory of Western bourgeois revolutions in modern times. Holding this banner, the bourgeoisie became the vanguard of the revolution opening up a new age. For countless ordinary people, they accepted the nascent bourgeois value system, which means they have also accepted the new era and new life. Regardless of the necessity conditions of survival, from the point of view of long-term survival and development, the above-mentioned values advocated by the bourgeoisie have undoubtedly become an inherent ideological power that guides the development of capitalist society, as well as the survival values that people follow and believe in. It is obvious that for hundreds of years, the civilization created by capitalism and the principles of thinking and conduct pursued by the people in the capitalist society are closely related to the dominant survival values in the capitalist society.

Chinese people are a group of people with wisdom of living and ideas of survival and development, for Chinese nation is a nation with long history, complex experiences and profound ideas. The famous American sociologist E. A. Ross, who had been living in China and profoundly observed the Chinese history and social life in the early twentieth century, once made such remarks on the Chinese people and Chinese nation:

> ... The races of the higher destiny are not so easily set in motion. They are able to hold back and digest their impulses. The key to their conduct is to be found, not in their impressions, but in their thoughts and convictions. Their course is to be interpreted not by their impulses but by their purposes. Their intellect is a massive fly-wheel by means of which continuous will power is derived from mixed and intermittent stimuli.[4]

These words of Ross are very reasonable, for what he saw is the source of power for the progress of a nation with the accumulation of history, thought and culture as well as a group of people with steady and reliable moral characters. In his opinion, the source of power lies in the stable thoughts and convictions. In simple words, such thoughts and convictions are actually the values that are owned by this nation and can be trusted and put into practice by the individuals.

For thousands of years, in the system of ideological values that the Chinese people believe in, the system of Confucian values is undoubtedly the most representative and typical. Since the country was unified in the Qin Dynasty and Confucianism unified people's ideology in the Han Dynasty, although there were invasion of new trends of thought sometimes, Confucianism has always occupied the dominant position in the ideological belief system of the Chinese. The morality that Confucianism advocates, in particular the values of "benevolence, righteousness, etiquette, wisdom and integrity", has been

> For thousands of years, in the system of ideological values that the Chinese people believe in, the system of Confucian values is undoubtedly the most representative and typical.

deeply imprinted in the minds and hearts of the Chinese people, guiding and determining their way of thinking and act. It has been a long time since the Confucian values were slowly established and then played a long-term role, and their influence is so far-reaching that they still fasten the minds and hearts of the Chinese in a loose manner like a chain that has not been completely broken as yet.

Things are changing all the time with the passage of time. For centuries, the enormous changes in Chinese society are not only a revolution in social formation, but also a revolution in ideology and culture. Since the beginning of the last century, under the guidance of the slogans of "democracy" and "science" proposed by the intellectual group who have foresight, Chinese people have always been exploring the road leading to the modernization in China. Chinese Communists have made outstanding contributions in leading Chinese revolution and promoting the modernization of Chinese society, among which one major contribution in ideology and culture is the spreading of the ideological beliefs of Marxism among the Chinese people. This is an extremely difficult undertaking with unprecedented troubles and challenges. Nowadays, the overall situation of the Chinese people's ideology and culture is the increasingly in-depth integration and complementation between Marxism as the state ideology and the Confucian tradition as secular values of the public as well as the Western thought as the trend of knowledge and culture. In addition to these, there still are a variety of other ideological and cultural trends that are also interacting and springing up.

Karl Marx and his *Das Kapital*

Under the influence of diverse trends of thought, the modern survival values of the Chinese are undoubtedly diversified. Among all survival values, we can list three dominant ones that are espoused by the majority of Chinese people:

The first is development. Development is precisely the values of "life" as we have mentioned above. What people think and do is always for a fundamental purpose— "life". Such a kind of "life" means both existence and development, which embodies not only the continuation of life, but also the success and acquisition in activities of life. In people's real life, their purposes and targets of survival can be developed, and people hope that their plans for survival can produce the desired effect and their actions can achieve the desired objectives. It can be said that development is the top priority in the survival values of the Chinese. In general, all the ideas and activities of people have the potential and the intention of development as long as they are consistent with the laws and principles of survival.

The second is harmony. Harmony is a distinct quality of Chinese thought and culture, which is also a consistent belief of the Chinese people. The ideas that "harmony is prized" and "harmony will lead to a prosperous population" espoused by the ancient Chinese people are still deeply rooted in the survival values of the modern Chinese people, for in Chinese people's minds, only harmony can create the optimal state of existence and the best environment for development. The harmony-oriented survival values are not only conducive to avoiding conflicts, eliminating contradictions and maximizing the balanced distribution of interests, but also helpful to maintaining existence and continuing development. One of the reasons why the concept of building a harmonious society is so popular and advocated by the majority of the masses of the people in modern China is that Chinese people have always had confidence in and hope for harmony, and respectfully regarded it as one of the most important survival values.

> Man cannot seize happiness; it is only by preserving a happy frame of mind that the essence of happiness can be summoned.

The third is happiness. Similar to development and harmony, happiness is also one of the important survival values of the Chinese, as well as a main value goal that Chinese people pursue in their activities of survival. German scholar Wolfgang Bauer once wrote a book on the subject of the view of happiness of the Chinese. He believes that

> China is a great country with great people. Maybe some would say that it has come to a ripe old age since it is born, like some legendary figures, but just for this reason, it is always renewing itself. It is asleep sometimes, but it never dies in sleep. In the four or five thousand years of history, it experienced all these forms of hopeful happiness with its own nature. [5]

In fact, for most ordinary people, the pursuit of happiness in their course of life is the most common value choice. Since ancient times, Chinese people have never placed too much emphasis on material wealth, but paid special attention to their inner feelings and spiritual needs when they are looking upon happiness. Of course, their inner wishes and spiritual needs are also limited. As the saying goes, "Man cannot seize happiness; it is only by preserving a happy frame of mind that the essence of happiness can be summoned."[6] Chinese people also often say "one should be content with what one is", which actually means to consciously restrain people's desires and needs, in case of the expansion of spiritual desire. This is the fundamental way for Chinese people to maintain and pursue happiness.

## 4. The View of Lifelong Learning of the Chinese

Learning is a way of survival, as well as an important means to improve the living conditions and obtain the opportunity of survival and development. Since ancient times, human beings have managed their survival and development in learning. In primitive society, human beings needed to maintain their survival by means of learning working and living skills as well as ways of overcoming natural difficulties. In their learning, they knew how to create and how to innovate, laying the foundation for the continuation and development of life. In class society, human beings need to learn the way of survival and development as well as the experience of innovation and progress from the practice of production, life and struggle. It can be said that the existence and development of human beings will never be separated from learning, otherwise, they will come to a standstill or even go backwards and fall to ruin. This is a plain and clear truth that has been proved by the common history of all the people regardless of their color, races, regions or social forms.

Learning is a way of survival, an attitude of life, and a key to progress. Shelley once said, the more we learn, the more we discover our ignorance. In the face of an entirely new thing or a totally unknown object, being able to hold a modest and studious attitude and using scientific and applicable means to turn the unknown to knowledge and solve the difficulties in thinking and cognition are, in fact, the manifestations of a powerful will of pursuing progress. In the history of human society, there are countless examples that have shown that all the people or groups good at learning are always able to maintain a positive, enterprising and progressive state, and win opportunities for development; whereas those that are poor at learning and live an idle life will eventually be eliminated.

Ancient Chinese people attached great importance to learning and thought much of lifelong learning. In their view, one's abilities will not be enhanced without learning, and only through constant learning, can one know what he is lacking in and what he is confused about; for this reason, they advocated an insatiable desire for learning, no end in learning, and constant reviewing or practicing of that already learnt. It should be said that this is a value judgment full of wisdom, because learning is a basic means to enhance one's talents, knowledge, wisdom and abilities, as well a practical way to ensure the survival, development and continuous reproduction of human beings. The sayings, proverbs and examples about valuing and advocating learning in China are too numerous to mention one by one, which is sufficient to prove that the fondness for learning and diligence in learning is an important ideological and cultural tradition in the Chinese society, as well as a habit that has been developed for a long time in the Chinese people's life. In this regard, there not only has been a consensus among Chinese people, but a lot of Westerners can also feel it. Domingo Navarrete, a missionary who had been living in China for 21 years in the 17th century, carefully examined the learning traditions of the Chinese nation and observed the learning habits of the Chinese people. He used two stories about Chinese people's pursuit of knowledge under difficulties to tell about the habit of loving learning of the Chinese people. Here, we excerpt a very detailed and vivid description by him as follows:

> One of the many advantages of Chinese schools is that there are very few play-days, there are not eight throughout the whole year, and no vacations at all. They are continually at it, and consequently there are men admirably versed in their laws history and morals, upon which they compose most ingenious and politic discourses, proved and adorned with all imaginable elegancy and learning. It would be wonderful if the scholars of Europe were like them, for they are the gravest, the most modest, and the most orderly people in China. So that when they see a Man in the street with his eyes fixed on the ground, and very modest, all men know

he is a student. The same earnestness and seriousness is seen even in school-boys. I often saw and observed this with no little surprise. The Chinese nation is much addicted to learning and inclined to reading. I have met men on the road in sedans or palanquins on men's shoulders, with a book in their hands. In cities I have often seen mandarins in the same manner. The tradesmen and shopkeepers sit behind their counters with books in front of them.[7]

Reader events at National Library of China

Chinese people regard learning as the way, condition and content of survival, which reflects a unique survival values. Such uniqueness can be shown in two aspects: from the secular perspective, from ancient China to today, learning is still an important means for Chinese people to improve living conditions, obtain job opportunities, and change their fates and way of survival. For example, a person, born poor and lowly, can change his status and fate by taking the imperial examination in ancient China, and today, learning still has a similar effect. To learn with the purpose of changing the fate and way of survival is the pragmatic side of the Chinese people in their pursuit of learning. From the spiritual perspective, Chinese people attach importance to the role of edification of culture, believing that learning, knowledge and culture can cultivate man's ideological and moral level, and improve the spiritual realm of man's existence and development.

In the spiritual pursuit of the Chinese people, the maximum value of survival is to attain "Dao" (or "Tao"). Dao is about the inherent laws of things and life, and the only way to attain "Dao" is through constant learning. "Dao" is profound and mysterious, thus the pursuit, learning and promotion of Dao is a long course without end. For this reason, the spiritual demands for learning to attain and promote Dao are lifelong and endless. The more Dao a man learns and the more Dao he promotes, the higher level of spiritualization he reaches and the higher realm of Dao he attains. If a man can pursue the law of spiritualization constantly, then it is deemed that the significance and value of his life has been realized and the goal of his life has been achieved. Of course, sometimes the most profound law just lies in the most simple life and things; however, it does not mean that to attain such laws need not to learn, but also requires profound understanding, extraordinary intelligence and great efforts in learning. And the acquisition of such laws can also bring people a sense of satisfaction and fulfillment.

Of course, in ancient China, for many intellectuals, the pursuit of fame and fortune, the pursuit of merits and achievements, and the pursuit of a family with prestige and honor might be their motivation for living and learning, and this, is the values of the majority of people who have secular pursuit as we have mentioned earlier. But, it is exactly such pursuit that stimulates many intellectuals to keep learning and make continuous efforts. Without doubt, this kind of learning cannot be regarded as the true lifelong learning, but is only a kind of reluctant and restricted learning with secular purposes. For this reason, a lot of people give up learning after achieving their secular goals, and then manage to live on in accordance with the stereotyped political and social system and order in China. And perhaps, the lack of encouragement and support in the stereotyped political and social system is precisely the limitation to study and learning in the Chinese tradition.

> Lifelong learning has become a mode of life and a way of survival, as well as a way of existence, in which man transcends the one-dimensional mode and achieves freedom and all-round development.

In modern Chinese ideological and cultural ideas, there is a far-reaching educational concept, that is, life is a process of endeavoring to progress and value can only be realized by creating. Such a view of value is not only the continuation of the conception of leaning in traditional Chinese values, but also the ideological foundation for the view of lifelong learning of modern people. Admittedly, the understanding of lifelong learning of modern Chinese people cannot completely get rid of the consideration of those secular goals in their lives; however, along with the improvement of people's living conditions, especially under the circumstances that people's physical and physiological needs such as the basic necessities have been no longer the key factor affecting human survival, people's pursuit of lifelong learning, to a large extent, has been promoted to a spiritual need. In the mind of modern people, lifelong learning has become a mode of life and a way of survival, as well as a way of existence, in which man transcends the one-dimensional mode and achieves freedom and all-round development.

In modern Chinese society, a circumstance where the lifelong education is valued and the lifelong learning is advocated has gradually formed. This, to a certain degree, should be credited to the Communist Party of China who has made great efforts in respect of ideas, policies, systems and practice for promoting the lifelong learning of the Chinese people. In 1993, the CPC Central Committee and the State Council issued the Outline of Education Reform and Development in China and for the first time formally proposed the concept of "lifelong education". In 1995 the NPC adopted the Education Law of the PRC, in which Article 11 provides: "The state shall fit in with the needs of the development of socialist market economy and the social progress, accelerate educational reform, promote the coordinated development of all kinds of education at all levels, establish and perfect the lifelong learning system." And Article 41 provides: "The state shall encourage schools, other educational institutions and social organizations to create conditions for the lifelong learning of citizens." On January 13, 1999, the State Council approved the Ministry of Education's Action Scheme for Invigorating Education Towards the 21st Century (promulgated on December 24, 1998), which pointed out that: "to gradually develop a lifelong learning system in an endeavor to enhance the quality of the whole nation", "by the year 2010… a lifelong learning system will be established". In May 2001, Jiang Zemin proposed that "we should construct a lifelong learning system and create a learning-oriented society". Since then, promoting the innovation in education system and gradually forming a learning-oriented society satisfying the needs of the lifelong learning, so as to meet the demands for the diversified learning of the masses has become an important strategy for the educational development and social construction of the Party and the State. In 2002, the Report to the 16th National Congress of the Communist Party of China stressed that: "A learning society in which all the people will learn or even pursue lifelong learning will emerge to boost their all-round development."[8] In 2007, the Report to the 17th National Congress of the Communist Party of China put forward again: "Distance learning and continuing education will be promoted to make ours a society in which every citizen is committed to learning and pursues lifelong learning."[9] In 2009, Chinese Vice President Xi Jinping, who is also Member of the Standing Committee of the Political Bureau of the CPC Central Committee and president of the Party School of the Communist Party of China Central Committee, systematically pointed out the importance of modern learning in his speech delivered at the opening ceremony of the Central Party School. He said that learning is the way of the inheritance of civilization, the ladder of the growth of life, the foundation for the consolidation of the Party, and the key to the prosperity of the State. This not only reflects the understanding of lifelong learning of the Chinese Communists, but also indicates the necessity and importance of strengthening lifelong learning for the contemporary Chinese people.

There are certain rules and also certain directions in the survival of mankind, and different nations and races will follow their own recognized rules and directions to create and then abide by different survival values. Chinese people are a group that believes in life, values life and cherishes life. In their survival values, the will to live is very strong and prominent. For the purpose of endless reproduction and development of life, Chinese people are learning and creating. In learning and creating, they created a brilliant history; and they are greeting a vibrant and bright future.

**Notes**

[1] *Mencius · Kao Tzu Part One*, Chapter X, Hohhot: Yuanfang Publishing House, 2007, p. 158.

[2] Ibid., pp. 158-159.

[3] Gustave Le Bon, *The Crowd: A Study of the Popular Mind*, Guilin: Guangxi Normal University Press, 2011, p. 5.

[4] E. A. Ross, *The Changing Chinese*, Beijing: Current Affairs Press, 1998, pp. 55-56.

[5] Wolfgang Bauer, *China and the Search for Happiness*, Nanjing: Jiangsu People's Publishing House, 2004, Preface, p. 5.

[6] Hong Yingming, *The Roots of Wisdom*, Hohhot: Yuanfang Publishing House, 2007, p. 40.

[7] Raymond Dawson, *The Chinese Chameleon: An Analysis of European Conceptions of Chinese Civilization*, Beijing: Current Affairs Press, 1999, p. 261. See the comments by Domingo Navarrete in the Appendix of the book.

[8] Jiang Zemin, *Build a Well-off Society in an All-Round Way and Create a New Situation in Building Socialism with Chinese Characteristics*, Beijing: People's Publishing House, 2002, p. 20.

[9] *Documents of the 17th National Congress of the Communist Party of China*, Beijing: People's Publishing House, 2002, p. 37.

# Chapter Three

# The State-supremacy Political Values

# 3 The State-supremacy Political Values

> Man is a political animal by nature.

Ancient Greek thinker Aristotle once said that man is a political animal by nature. This statement, in fact, points out the basic attribute of human being as a political man, and also shows man's special nature of being an organized social and political group. Engaging in political activities is a choice of being socialized of human beings as a social group, which began as early as in the clan society. The Chinese nation is a group that formed state system and political institution very early in the world civilization system, and it has experienced dozens of dynastic changes and thousands of political struggles in its long course of historical development, therefore, Chinese people are no stranger to politics at all. Even since very long time ago, Chinese people have begun to care about politics, talk about politics and participate in politics. In *The Analects*, a famous classic work of the Chinese nation, there are a lot of records of discussing and participating in politics. Owing to the special social organization and political development order, the traditional Chinese society always applies an organizational model that family and country share a common organizational structure, and thereby the State-supremacy political values was formed and followed by the Chinese people.

## 1. Cultivating the People, Regulating the Family, Governing and Pacifying the Country

Speaking of the political values of the Chinese, the starting point of thinking that needs to be grasped most is the concept of family and the concept of country in Chinese society. In the long traditional society,

> Treat all families as your own family and treat all countries as your own country.

there formed a thinking mode and conception that family and country share a common organizational structure and are integrated together; therefore, in their understanding of the relationship between family and country, Chinese people tend to treat them as a whole, and never make a strict distinction between them, not to mention set them against one another in an absolute manner. Moreover, in the mind of the Chinese people, the essence of politics is inseparable from the governance of family and country; so, in understanding their political values, we need to proceed from the relationship between family and country and should not in the least ignore the priority and order of family and country in their mind. Among the numerous well-known sayings that are still popular until today, many mention the relationship between family and country in Chinese people's mind, of which the most famous one is that "treat all families as your own family and treat all countries as your own country" mentioned in *Guan Zi • On Governing the People*, which not only expresses a view on a broad-minded patriotism, but also makes people directly perceive the relationship between family and country in the mind of the Chinese.

In the celebration activities for the 60th anniversary of the PRC in 2009, there was a song entitled "The Country and the Family", and the main part of its lyrics is as follows:

> What is a country, what is a family; all say a country is very big, it is actually a family; I fill my country in my heart, I support my family with my hands; a family is the smallest country, a country is thousands of families. There is my country in the world,

there is my family on earth; only my country is powerful, can my family be rich.

This song expresses the true feelings of the Chinese people and also represents the relationship between country and family in the thought and value system of the Chinese people.

In the mind of the Chinese people, the family is a very sweet home, and it is also a concept full of tender sentiments. As we have mentioned earlier, the traditional Chinese character of family or home represents that people live together with livestock under roofs, which, in fact, reflects the origin of the concept of family in Chinese people's mind, that is, living under the same roof, where there are people and livestock, and the roof can shelter them from the wind and rain, so that they can live a comfortable and easy life in their homes. Naturally this will make people have a desire to approach and embrace the home, for it is a place representing ease, safety and family. It can be said that for Chinese people, home is the most real and warmest place for man's subsistence. The traditional Chinese character of country comprises the population and the borders that stand for territory, which actually is an extension of the concept of "family", in other words, a country is exactly a political community where numerous families are organized together to form such substantial factors as population and land and are combined together to play a role of safeguarding. Therefore, in the eyes of the Chinese people, the country and the family are inseparable. The generally used word "country" are often translated as "国家" (country and family), and Chinese people themselves also often use "国" and "家" together and seldom separate them.

In ancient China, the territory dominated by a monarch is called a "country" and the fief dominated by a vassal is called a "family". The title of vassal is conferred by the monarch, and in the early period, the feudal lords are often the relatives or family members of the monarch, thus not only in terms of kinship, they have close relationship with the monarch, but also in respect of political subordination and management system, even those have less close kinship are still inseparable from the monarch. The monarch holds the absolute power over everything, including one's life, property and rank or position. Therefore, the "family" represented by the vassal is greatly dependent on the "country" represented by the monarch, thus leading to the thinking prototype of the inseparability of country and family in the traditional concept of the Chinese people.

In fact, it is the origin and organizational mode that determine the characteristics of the Chinese family structure. In ancient times, people's ability to use and control nature was not high due to the low level of productivity and social life, they needed to collaborate collectively and support each other in the social production, so that they were able to maintain their common survival and development. Apart from the simple labor, those social production activities that are a bit more complex will rely on the organized cooperation of many people. Therefore, the co-production and association between people become a necessity, and on the basis of the consanguinity as well as public and cooperative social production, the original family relationship and social organizations were constructed. With the expansion of the scale of social production and the family relationship, people gradually brought larger society organizations into the range of production and life and expanded the space of production and life based on them. After the slavery countries were set up, primitive tribe and clan system were disintegrated, and the concept of the organized and socialized family was formed and developed, thereby the family constituted the social unit of the country, providing the foundation in terms of social organization for the development of social production and the rule of ruling class. As the feudal society was formed, the development of the social productivity and the promotion of the feudality further reinforced the fact that the family is the basic social organization and the constituent unit of the country. However, although the family is further separated from the monarchy, imperial power and state system, the family and the country are still always linked together.

In the thought of the people in traditional society, the family refers to their own families, and the country is a collection of political power that contains many families, that is, a collection of countless families, in general, it refers to the vassal state, whereas the world is a broader country that includes many vassal states, that is, a united world. The emperor who has the supreme authority is the greatest king in the broad world, what he has is the imperial power, and he is also known as "Huang Shang" (literally Emperor Highness), for his status is higher than all the people. The family in the eyes of the emperor is the whole world, including all families, land, population and resources. In order to realize the supremacy of his power, the emperor claims that he comes to govern and manage the world on behalf of Heaven, and because his status is only lower than Heaven, he declares himself to be the "Son of Heaven", and refers to himself as "Zhen" to show that he is the spokesman of Heaven. For ordinary people, the notion from the family to the country and then the world is expanding and upgrading step by step, in which it contains the Self but also transcend the Self, and it contains the subordination but also progressively transcend the subordination. The one dominant in a family will become an inferior before a vassal, and a vassal will become a subordinate of the emperor. In light of this, there forms a network of superior-subordinate relations between people owing to their different social relations, and the supreme emperor is in the very center of this network, for him, "everything under the heaven obeys the emperor's command and everywhere within the boundaries are the emperor's land".

Red Lanterns reflect happiness (CNSPHOTO)

Because of such relationships, there is order between people, and the moral order is the ethics. In accordance with the order of family, country and world: in a family, there are family ethics, that is, the principles of

> The father is affectionate and the son is filial, the husband assumes responsibilities and the wife has female virtues, the elder is friendly and the younger is respectful.

thinking and conduct of treating clan relatives, parents, brothers and sisters, sons and daughters and later generations. In the traditional society, Chinese people are used to believing that the basic family ethics are "the father is affectionate and the son is filial, the husband assumes responsibilities and the wife has female virtues, the elder is friendly and the younger is respectful". Just because in the mind of the Chinese people, the country is essentially a big family and in the traditional society, the patriarch of this family is actually the monarch who has the supreme power, the monarch as the greatest patriarch enjoys the loyalty of the whole world. And what he should grant to his subjects is the greatest kindness; this is what is called "the monarch is kind and the subject is loyal". In a society beyond the family, there are social ethics, that is, the morals of treating neighbors, friends, others and the world. Such morals are reflected not only in the professional life of a person, but also in his association with other social members, including both professional ethics and public morality, in which the basic requirements are "benevolence, righteousness, etiquette, wisdom and integrity". These social values in forms of ethics and morality are binding on the order of people's daily lives as well as their way of act, and their basic goal is to achieve the harmony, stability, happiness and prosperity inside and outside the family and the country. To this end, those men who are ambitious and capable of great achievements need to transcend the Self in moral sense in pursuit of a greater realm of life and complete a transition from the family to the country so as to realize the moral ideals and political ideals, that is, "cultivating the people, regulating the family, governing the country and pacifying the world". In such a pursuit of life that combines moral ideals and political ideals together, the family and the country are united, and the politics in the family and in the country are rooted in the same ethical norms.

Due to the close relationship between family and country, the ethical values reflected in the Chinese family is not just a moral value, but also a political value. Because, the concept of treating the people, society and world contained in family will greatly affect and to some extent, determine Chinese people's attitude towards political organizations, political order and political system. Under the impact of economic globalization, both the concept of family ethics and the concept of country of the modern Chinese people have undergone changes. The younger generation in the social transformation will no longer view the relationship between family and country in accordance with the traditional way of thinking or stubbornly abide by the political and moral ideals of "cultivating the people, regulating the family, governing the country and pacifying the world" as the ancients. However, no matter what changes occurred in Chinese society and no matter how much impact the economic interests have on the traditional values, in the concept of the modern Chinese people, the family and the country are still very important objects of value, their love for family and country are still the survival sentiments that they can never part with. And the personal morality, family morality, professional and social ethics suitable for the modern social life are still the ethical value pursuit that the Chinese people advocate, praise and strive to practice.

## 2. Patriotism and Internationalism

In the traditional Chinese thought and culture, there is a concept that the family and the country are consistent and governing the country and governing the world are united, therefore, for the Chinese people, the love of country and the love of people or things other than country are united. In other words, the Chinese people can equally treat their own country and the world outside their country by placing them at the same level of value, and give their same passionate and rational love to them. This is an important feature of the Chinese in treating the problems of patriotism and internationalism, and such feature has existed since the ancient times and becomes more distinct in today's era of economic globalization.

During the period of slave-owning society in China, there were many vassal states, and the vassals were representatives of the supreme power in their domains, so, the patriotism advocated at that time is actually equivalent to the loyalty, that is, to treat the vassals themselves with the supreme loyalty. "Before the Qin and Han dynasties, Han people and the Chinese nation were still in gestation. People of Qin, Chu, Wu and Yue... had not yet become a part of ancient China, People of Qin built Qin, People of Wu built Wu... all peoples were loyal to their own countries (vassal states) and served their own masters."[1] However, even in this period, Chinese people's concept of the "world" had already formed; many people took the "world" as the object of their love, instead of separately regarding some one vassal state as the only object of their love. Along with the formation of feudalism and the continuous integration of many ethnic groups, a united state power was developed and consolidated, and the concept of patriotism of the Chinese was also renewing with the change of times. From the resistance to enemy invasion to the maintenance of the unity of territory and sovereignty, from the opposition to colonialism to the opposition to feudalism, Chinese people's patriotism has different meanings at different times. Regardless of the change of the meanings of patriotism, Chinese people's patriotic ideas and sentiments will be always reflected as their love for homeland and culture, their obedience to orders and norms, as well as their broad mind of devoting themselves to, benefiting and caring for the people all over the world without being restricted to the boundaries, while virtuously conducting themselves.

Of course, it is undoubtedly naive, or even undue and unreasonable to require all the Chinese people, especially the authorities in traditional Chinese society to have to treat all countries in the world in the same way with their own people and dependencies. Since modern times, China has been forced to enter into the outside world from the state of seclusion, to re-examine the modern Western countries and the Western world, and to build up a new and undesired relationships. At this time, the patriots who remained sober-minded appealed to the people to protect the rights and interests, territory and resources of China through the anti-imperialist struggle; the patriotism like this is reasonable. As what the American missionary Holcombe Chester said, "That she should resent what, from her standpoint, was an unwarranted intrusion, is but natural."[2] In fact, before the modern countries and the Chinese people's national consciousness were formed, the value orientation of the Chinese people of longing for peace, pursuing peace and avoiding war is very obvious, and their concept of love for peace has been recognized by many people who traveled in China and had deep knowledge of China. Such values of advocating, valuing and pursuing peace is not only an expression of patriotism, but without doubt also an expression of internationalism.

Since the modern times, in the significant social revolutions taken place in China, patriotism has been given new meanings and spirit. In the early twentieth century, along with the rise of the world proletarian revolutionary movement, Chinese revolutionaries were able to observe the problem of social change in China from a world revolutionary perspective. Determined by the special class and political nature of the proletarian revolutionary movement, it is necessary that the proletariat will rely on and unite with the proletariat of the world in carrying out their domestic revolutionary movement, thus constituting the revolutionary alliance of the proletariat and forging their internationalist sentiments. As a matter of fact, the proletarian revolution itself is a cosmopolitan and transnational revolution, and the self-liberation movement that the proletariat of a country is engaged in itself is also a part of the world proletarian revolutionary movement, therefore the patriotism and internationalism advocated by the proletariat are inseparable. And this point has been demonstrated rather obviously in the New Democratic Revolution in China. Mao Zedong mentioned the patriotic mission of the Chinese Communist and Chinese people many times, and also stressed the internationalist duty. He said,

> Can a Communist, who is an internationalist, at the same time, be a patriot? We hold that he not only can be but must be. ...Chinese Communists must therefore combine patriotism with internationalism. We are at once internationalists and patriots. Thus in wars of national liberation, patriotism is applied internationalism.[3]

This argument actually set up an important principle that guides the proletarian revolution in China, and also became a major category that affects the concept of national politics of the Chinese people.

Along with the process of China's modernization, Chinese people's modern national consciousness has been constructed. In the minds of modern Chinese people, the country is no longer the private property that belongs to some "Son of Heaven" or specifically possessed by some royal family as in the past, but a political community owned by all the Chinese people, as well as a machine of implementing people's democratic dictatorship, of which the working people are masters. Since the country in the modern sense is not an illusory community as what some political commentators declare, but a systematic structure with specific political system, ideology and social organization, the so-called patriotism of modern people cannot be divorced from the actual content of a country. Mainly speaking, the patriotism in present times is inseparable from the political party, ethnic group, society, as well as the current political and economic patterns, social system and ideology. That is to say, the patriotism of the modern Chinese people is impossible to break away from China's national conditions and reality, in particular, the state system, political system and social system in China. In fact, patriotism, in any country and in any era, is not abstract or unreal, but has specific content and ideological principles. Any patriotism based on some historical moment in the past or some development trend in the imagined future is unrealistic and impractical.

In fact, patriotism, in any country and in any era, is not abstract or unreal, but has specific content and ideological principles.

In contemporary China, the tide of economic globalization has influenced and changed Chinese people's understanding of history and culture in many ways. In fact, not only in China, but also in many countries and regions in the world, a strong consciousness of "cultural uprootness" is spreading and eroding people's traditional ideas. A lot of people, especially the younger generation tend to look upon and analyze the existing national framework of international relations with a transnational consciousness. Under such circumstances, it seems that those objects and events originally within the category of patriotism may be challenged by the tendency of internationalism. And the boundary and relationship between patriotism and internationalism in people's minds will be also changed in their value judgments and choices. However, the Chinese people have already unified the patriotic values and the internationalist values well since the modern times, therefore, for the contemporary Chinese people, there always remains a space of internationalism in their patriotic ideas, and they will never lose the internationalist sentiments at the time of advocating patriotism.

When it comes to the topic of patriotism and internationalism, we have to pay attention to a special group of people—overseas Chinese. From a very early time, many Chinese people have gone abroad and made their living there. After the mid-nineteenth century, lots of Chinese people went to and earned their living in Southeast Asia. After the reform and opening up, more Chinese people immigrated to foreign countries. Up to today, we really cannot count the number of overseas Chinese and the number of Chinese people in all countries of the world. There is a vivid and popular saying that "where there are people living and acting, there are Chinese people". Since there are so many Chinese that are living abroad or even have acquired foreign

## 我的中国心

黄 霑 词
王福龄 曲

My Chinese Heart

citizenship, then what is the concept of patriotism and internationalism like in their minds? This question is actually related to the problem about the border of patriotism and involved with a hot issue that is studied in today's international academic circles—Trans Nation.

For those overseas Chinese, as well as the group of people living abroad, it is hard for us to look upon and understand them with the traditional concept of patriotism. In their minds, no matter where they live and no matter what nationalities they have, their native land must still remain in their hearts. In the 1980s, there was an upsurge of going abroad, and there was also a popular song once sweeping China and the world—*My Chinese Heart* sung by Zhang Mingmin. The lyric reads: "Although Western outfits dress me, my heart will always be Chinese." This is the common voice of many overseas Chinese, as well as their expression of patriotic values!

## 3. A View of State Governance by the Use of both Law and Morality

Throughout history, many countries will uphold certain views of State governance, and there are a variety of views of State governance. The State cannot be separated from politics, and it is the major representation of politics, therefore the view of State governance of a country will necessarily reflect certain political values. In any social formation, there will be phenomenon of unequal possession and uneven distribution in terms of politics, political power and state power; therefore in general, it is always the case that those holding state power control the initiative in State governance, and they also can always upgrade their values of State governance to the dominant position. Through long-term social governance and ideological indoctrination, such a dominant view of State governance will become the acceptable values, and such values will be used to constrain the behavior of groups.

Tutorship by young volunteer (CNSPHOTO)

In Chinese history, the traditional sense of State was originated very early, and there was a lot of thinking on the political ideas and principles of State governance, therefore a well-developed concept of State governance was formed in a very early time. During the Xia, Shang and Zhou dynasties, the slavery in China experienced a process from formation to prosperity and then to decline, and it was also a period of exploration and formation of the concept of State governance in early China. Since a long time has passed and the time span between the three dynasties is also very long, together with the small amount of the documents and materials that still exist; today, we can only roughly describe the basic concept of traditional State governance in the ancient China by virtue of some accounts of later generations. A general characteristic of this concept is that although different dynasties have their own dominant core concepts of State governance, their basic approach is to highlight either the rule of law or the rule of morality, in which sometimes morality takes priority over law;

sometimes the heavy punishment and severe law are implemented and the rule of morality is relaxed, but in general, both the rule of law and the rule of morality are implemented without coming into conflict.

In the two strategies of State governance—the rule of law and the rule of morality, the latter is preventive and prerequisite, as for the former, although it can fulfill the purpose of controlling crimes and maintaining social stability by exerting its deterrent effect and enforcing power, it is after all still restrictive and punitive. So, in the governance of a country, if the goal can be achieved by the rule of morality, we should prudentially resort to the rule of law and avoid using the authority of law to subdue others. In the Volume 52 of *The History of Latter Han*, there is a paragraph of description about the ancient emperors' view of State governance:

> The ancient emperors take law and morality as the bit and take officials as the rein and whip, the man good at horse riding will put the bit at the right place, fully prepare the rein and whip, appropriately use the power of horses and make horses pull together, in this way, he can drive thousands of miles without yelling. The man good at managing people will unify law and morality, put officials at the right place, appropriately use the power of people, set people's minds at rest; therefore, the world will be governed without using punishment.

This paragraph not only mentions the view of State governance by the use of both law and morality, but also puts forward the idea of giving priority to the rule of morality in governing the State.

Like any country in other types of civilization, the ancient Chinese society and dynasties are disposed to adopt a certain kind of concept of State governance in governing the State, either placing extra emphasis on the rule of morality or the rule of law. Generally speaking, in the turbulent times, the State tends to use severe punishment, whereas in flourishing age, it often resorts to the rule of morality. However, comparatively speaking, in the over two thousand years of imperial rule in traditional Chinese society, the rule of morality is a bit more, and people's appeals for and emphasis on it are also a bit more. Of course, in Chinese feudal society, many virtues in respect of interpersonal relationships and social intercourse had been set up in a very early time; therefore the appeals for these virtues actually become a reflection of the view of the rule of morality.

During the Spring and Autumn Period, Guan Zhong, a politician of Qi, put forward many principles for State governance, of which, a feature is to stress the rule of morality. He said that etiquette, righteousness, honesty, and sense of shame are the four principles of a state, if they are not implemented, the state will be ruined. The etiquette, righteousness, honesty, and sense of shame mentioned here are then already-formed virtues for the State governance. After Guan Zhong, Confucius and Mencius who established and carried forward Confucianism put more emphasis on the rule of morality. For example, Confucius said:

> If the people are led by laws, and uniformity sought to be given them by punishments, they will try to avoid the punishment, but have no sense of shame. If they are led by virtue, and uniformity sought to be given them by the rules of propriety, they will have the sense of shame, and moreover will become good.

If the people are led by laws, and uniformity sought to be given them by punishments, they will try to avoid the punishment, but have no sense of shame. If they are led by virtue, and uniformity sought to be given them by the rules of propriety, they will have the sense of shame, and moreover will become good. (*The Analects* • *Book 2*)

Mencius advocated that the monarch should implement the policy of benevolence and practice benevolent government. He said, if the monarch runs a government benevolent to the people and sparing of punishments and fines, the purpose that the State is prosperous and the people are strong will ultimately be achieved. Before and after the Qin Dynasty unified China, the concept of State governance of Han Fei, Li Si and other representatives of Legalist was valued; therefore Qin Dynasty laid more stress on the thought of Legalist in the governance of the State. However, in the two thousand years of time after that, the combination and mutual complement of the concepts of the rule of law and the rule of morality has become a view of State governance that is accepted by the Chinese society.

The rule of law and the rule of morality should be applied together, and it is hard to fully realize the perfect governance of the State by any of them alone.

The experience in State governance accumulated in the long-term traditional Chinese society tells us that the rule of law and the rule of morality should be applied together, and it is hard to fully realize the perfect governance of the State by any of them alone. In view of the general situation around the world, owing to the increasingly complex social and international relations, the State governance in modern times become more complex and difficult than ever before, and there are also much more emergencies need to be dealt with and responded to. Since the reform and opening up, China marches forward on the road of promoting the reform of the socialist market economy and has made remarkable achievements that attracted worldwide attention. In essence, the socialist market economy is an economic system under the rule of law, which can only be effectively realized and play its role by dint of the legal protection and support. However, a prominent feature of the market economy is interest-oriented, and the way to realize it is to promote people's freedom, initiative and enthusiasm in the creation of economic, political and cultural interests through the changes in system, mechanism and order; besides, there are huge conflicts of interest under the conditions of market economy, therefore the harmony, stability and development of the society are not only in need of a strong and effective guarantee from the rule of law, but also require a perfect guarantee from the rule of morality. The rule of law is a tough means, which resorts to the compulsion of law to restrict people's thoughts, words and deeds and build a "perimeter" and "floor" that cannot be exceeded, so as to avoid and punish crimes; while the rule of morality is a soft means, which resorts to the power of morality to restrict people's thoughts, words and deeds and construct a spiritual order, so as to improve peoples' character. Therefore, the rule of law and the rule of morality should be both applied and integrated together, and should be complementary and indispensable to each other.

The traditional families in China mostly practice the patriarchal system, in a family, the position of the father or the mother is very special and important, they work hard to raise their children, and also feel that it is their bounden duty to choose and plan for the future of their children. In the traditional family values, the father should be strict and the mother should be kind, the father often represents norms and laws, whereas the mother represents etiquette and virtue. It can be said that the traditional Chinese family is exactly a miniature model of a country that adheres to the combination and unity of the rule of law and the rule of morality, as well as a miniature of the concept of the Chinese people who link the governance of the State and the governance of the family together. Traditional Chinese society values etiquette and social relationship, thereby forming a relationship based society with emphasis on association between acquaintances and interpersonal contacts. In the process of nurturing and developing the socialist market economy, etiquette norms and social relationships not only can exert their beneficial effects of teaching people to be good, but also may bring about adverse effects to the new social norms and market order and hold back the construction of the modern social relationships, thus the key is how to guide, control and use these norms and relationships.

Under the influence of the long-term historical thought and culture, there is no lack of genes of the rule of law and the rule of morality in the values of the modern Chinese people. Moreover, through the nurturing and development in over thirty years of reform and opening up and decades of socialist market economy with Chinese characteristics, the Party and the Government place more and more emphasis on the importance of the use of both the rule of law and the rule of morality in the State governance and social construction in China, and more and more Chinese people are increasingly aware of the importance of the balance between the rule of law and the rule of morality in the State governance, which is specifically manifested as: since the reform and opening up, all aspects of social management and State governance in China are constantly improving their legal systems, mechanisms and norms and they are all progressing in line with the principle of governing the country by law in a sound manner, besides, people's consciousness of the rule of law, and the abidance by law are increasingly strengthened. Meanwhile, people become more concerned about the problem of social morality and individual morality under the conditions of the socialist market economy and they are in more urgent need of building a benign moral environment and better moral life. In addition, people's awareness, ability and level of reflecting on and digging for the root causes of some social events and issues after their occurrence are also greatly enhanced.

## 4. A View of International Association Advocating Equality, Peace and Harmony

Modern Chinese people are upholding a view of international association that advocates equality, peace and harmony. Such a view was originated in the concept of "natural harmony" that Chinese people rely on and try hard to cultivate, and not only in the modern era, but as early as in traditional Chinese society it has already become the major values of the Chinese. The old Chinese saying goes, "In practicing the rules of propriety, it is harmony that is prized. This is what is so precious in the ways of the ancient kings", "harmony will lead to a prosperous population", "within the four seas are all brothers", and so forth, are all the manifestations of the concepts of treating others as equals and valuing harmony that Chinese people emphasize. This concept deeply influenced and shaped the view of international association of modern Chinese people, making them always take equality, peace and harmony as the highest value goals and regard the realization of equality and peace as the ultimate international ethics in their international association.

Chinese people have a broad and open-minded "world" concept, which is closely related with the vastness of China's territory. From the perspective of ethnic relations and regime development, the history of the formation and development of the whole Chinese nation as well as the evolution of Chinese society is actually a history that all ethnic groups are integrated with each other and renew themselves in the integration. For thousands of years, there were dozens of dynasties rising and falling in the land of China, and there were hundreds of regional regimes and kingdoms established by the various ethnic minorities. Although in some times and some dynasties, some rulers also held the prejudice, like hostility and contempt or even the wrong concept that "all aliens are sure to be of a different heart", against foreigners; in most dynasties and periods, the rulers of the central regime were able to treat the regional regimes of minorities and the vassal states of other races with a open mind. And in some historical periods, some feudal rulers might also hold that only the central regimes in their hands are orthodox and reasonable, while those regional regimes and vassal states scattered around should all submit to the central regime; for this reason, they might wage wars against them, these wars were mostly within the scope of the territory of China. In view of the laws of the history of human society and regime development, it can be found that these short, interior and regional wars are inevitable and not uncommon in other countries in the world. They are most limited to the replacement of internal regime and kingship in China, which have no influence on the view of peaceful international association held by the Chinese people.

> If any nation in the world could ever be "too proud to fight", that nation would be China. The natural Chinese attitude is one of tolerance, friendliness, and courtesy.

The view of advocating equality, peace and harmony of the Chinese people is reflected not only in their life, work and daily intercourse, but also in their handling of international relations and international affairs. For Westerners, they get no access to the values of advocating equality, peace and harmony of the Chinese until they fully understand China and the Chinese people. However, once they have lived in China or get along with the Chinese people for a long time, they will deeply feel the value orientation of advocating equality, peace and harmony of the Chinese people and also understand Chinese people's firm pursuit of equality, peace and harmony. In the first chapter of this book, we have mentioned the views of China of those Westerners who traveled, preached and worked in China in the last few hundred years, most of whom stayed or lived in China for a long time and can fully understand the view of advocating equality, peace and harmony of the Chinese people. According to incomplete statistics, almost 90 percent Westerners who lived in China once mentioned the submissive and humble side in Chinese people's minds and characters in their works, and most Westerners recognize that Chinese nation value harmony very much and treat others as equals. In this regard, just to take a glance at those alien works about the view of China that we mentioned in this book, you will find sufficient evidence. Here, we just cite some words of the well-known British thinker Russell as an illustration.

In the early 1920s, Russell once visited China and delivered some speeches, and wrote the famous *The Problem of China* to express his view on the Chinese civilization, Chinese society, Chinese nation and Chinese people. He said, "If any nation in the world could ever be 'too proud to fight', that nation would be China. The natural Chinese attitude is one of tolerance, friendliness, and courtesy." Such argument is the best reflection of the Chinese people's view of advocating equality, peace and harmony in international association.

Bertrand Russell

The view of international association of the contemporary Chinese people has the inward and outward performance of practice: from the perspective of domestic situations, contemporary China adheres to a new road of peaceful development, committing itself to achieving the purpose that the country is prosperous and the people are strong in a peaceful situation. This is a requirement of all the Chinese people as well as the aspiration of the Party and the Government in China. From the perspective of international situations, as China grows stronger, the Chinese people will take a more high-spirited, confident and open-minded attitude towards the world; and China also will pay more attention to the peace and harmony of the world and persist in making contributions to the building of a harmonious world with durable peace and common prosperity. In April 2006, Chinese President Hu Jintao delivered a speech entitled "Promoting Peace in the Middle East and Building a Harmonious World" at the Consultative Council of the Kingdom of Saudi Arabia. In the speech such core words as "respect", "equality", "fairness", "peace", "dialogue", "negotiation" and "cooperation" frequently appeared, which fully express the view of international association that advocates equality, peace and harmony pursued by China and the Chinese people and clearly represents China's efforts and resolutions of adhering to the road of peaceful development and the building of a harmonious world.

> Peaceful development is the wisdom of the Chinese people, the pursuit of the Chinese people, and it can also bring happiness and peace to the people of the world.

Throughout history, the reality has proved beyond doubt that the road of peaceful development followed by China can benefit the Chinese people and the people of the world. Peaceful development is the wisdom of the Chinese people, the pursuit of the Chinese people, and it can also bring happiness and peace to the people of the world. The economic miracle occurred in China since the reform and opening up has enabled millions of Chinese people to get rid of poverty and get on to the road to wealth and happiness. Just in terms of the eradication of poverty, China has made a remarkable contribution to the world, and its contributions in other aspects brought by the road of peaceful development will also be increasingly known, understood, recognized and approved by more and more people in the world.

**Notes**

[1] Wu Xiongwu, *The Spirit of the Chinese Nation*, Kunming: Yunnan Nationalities Publishing House, 2004, p. 118.

[2] Holcombe Chester, *Real Chinaman*, Beijing: Guangming Daily Press, 1998, p. 12.

[3] *Selected Works of Mao Tse-tung*, Vol. II, Beijing: People's Publishing House, 1991, pp. 520~521.

# The Values of the Chinese

THE VALUES OF THE CHINESE
THE VALUES OF THE CHINESE

Chapter Four

# The Beneficial Economic Values

# 4 The Beneficial Economic Values

We are all pretty familiar with the word "economy", which generally refers to the business and creative production activities. In China, people often use the wording of "Jing Bang Ji Shi", which basically means that a man manages, develops and utilizes the objective world where he and others coexist through his activities in an objectified manner, so as to achieve the purpose of benefiting the people, the society and the world. People's life and survival are inseparable from the economic activities of transforming the nature, developing resources, creating wealth and promoting social development, and thereby their basic understanding and value judgment of economic life constitute the economic values. In people's values system, economic values are very important values, which reflect the value of people's economic activities, especially the basic concept of utilizing the nature and exploitable resources. All socialized nations and groups will hold the view on the objects in the outside world as well as their utilization; of course Chinese people are no exception.

It is an effective way to observe the ideological characteristics of a group or a nation from the point of view of economic values, for the creative activities of any group or any nation will be associated with its economic values. It can be even believed that we can see something directly related to the basic and common life pursuit that a group, a nation or a social community holds from its economic values. Therefore, from the economic values of the Chinese people, we can see their ways to understand the relationship between man and various substances, resources and factors in the objective world, as well as their attitudes, thoughts and action in treating the objects in the outside world.

## 1. Have the Chinese People Become Economic Animals?

The "economic animal" is a phrase for the description of a nation, a group or a social community, which is often used in oral expression, and today, it has become a basic terminology in the sociological study. In the 1970s and 1980s, Western economists called the Japanese who were busy creating economic benefits and worked so hard the "economic animals". It was at that time when Japanese economy grew rapidly and Japan just shook off the trauma caused by the Second World War, then became an economic powerhouse in the world that the Japanese were accompanied by this appellation. Therefore apparently, it is a pejorative remark, but actually, there is no lack of praise for the Japanese people's diligence, respect of work, and courage to strive and compete. Coincidentally, over thirty years later, a report entitled "A Group of 'Economic Animals' in Flourishing China" was published on March 11, 2010 in Singapore's *Lianhe Zaobao*, it holds that after the reform and opening up, China is in a flourishing time, but there also appears "a group of economic animals" who are wealthy but arrogant, extravagant, licentious, idle, unkind and worship money.

In May 2012, someone also issued an article "Chinese People Win the Title of 'Economic Animals'" in his blog, which said something similar with *Lianhe Zaobao* and also disclosed the fact that some foreign media called Chinese People "economic animals". However, the "economic animals" mentioned here lacks the tone of praise set on the Japanese, but is full of hostility as well as the sentiments of criticism and disdain. In fact, in recent years, many foreigners have misunderstandings about the values of pursuing economic development of the Chinese people and regard them as machines of interests that know nothing but making money and see nothing but money. Well, have Chinese people really become economic animals that worship money and economic interests? And what kind of economic values do modern Chinese people hold? For such questions, it is necessary to make some clarification and explanation.

Since the reform and opening up, China is committed to the building and development of the socialist market economy. Since the market economy is interest-oriented, it can, to the utmost extent, mobilize the enthusiasm and initiative of people in their economic development and social production. Through decades of policy guidance and institutional constraint, there's no doubt that more and more Chinese people become increasingly willing to participate in economic activities, engage in economic development, and promote economic utilization consciously. In people's real social life, economic criteria are more broadly used for the evaluation of their work performance, creative ability and behavior level than in the past. People often use one's income including his gains from wage, investment, business, production and management to evaluate his ability in economic activity. Just because of such changes in people's consciousness, a part of the Chinese people who get rich earlier owing to various opportunities and conditions, especially those groups getting rich quickly become the "economic animals" with the characteristics of worshiping money and economic interests, as we have mentioned above. In this sense, the description of these people in the report and blog is not totally unreasonable.

However, it should be noted that, although the market economy has changed the concept of market, economy and some aspects of life of the Chinese people, the economic value is not the sole criterion for the contemporary Chinese people's observation and analysis of all social life and production activities, nor are money and economic interests the only basis for their survival. Compared to the past, people's sense of efficiency, sense of competition and concept of interest have significantly enhanced, but in the values system of the contemporary Chinese people, economic interests and money are not the only things. On the contrary, the more developed the economy is and the more prominent the material interests are, the more emphasis will be put on the political, cultural, moral and other non-economic factors. Furthermore, even if there are indeed some people who have been subject to economic interests and money and become the "economic animals" described in the articles, this part of "economic animals" cannot be representative of all the Chinese people, and some of their purely economic behavior is of individuality and locality, which can either not represent the economic values of all the Chinese people. In light of this, it is obviously incorrect to regard all the Chinese people as "economic animals".

To judge whether or not some economic interests are desirable and feasible is in need of a comprehensive analysis, the concept that "one size fits all" should be avoided. Sima Qian, a Chinese historiographer of the Western Han Dynasty, once said in his *Historial Records • Biographies of Businessmen* that "all the people bustling in the world go after profits". It is often used to show the profit-seeking nature of people's thought and behavior, and also used as an excuse for some profit-making behavior nowadays. Although this sentence clearly points out that people always have a profit-seeking nature since ancient times, in fact, it is still mainly to describe the prosperous situation of people's economic activities. From the perspective of human nature, valuing interests is one kind of value pursuit of human beings, and also, going after profits and avoiding disadvantages is one of their natures. Under certain social conditions, the key to determine whether or not the interests, especially economic interests, are desirable does not lie in whether or not people seek interests, but in whether or not the interests they seek are healthy, and whether or not the values behind their behavior of seeking interests are proper, reasonable and beneficial to the overall development and coordinated progress of the society.

Since the reform and opening up till today, it is true that Chinese people pay more emphasis on material interests and income distribution than in the past, they become more enthusiastic about striving for economic interests and material conditions, and their sense of competition, fairness, creativity and market also have been greatly enhanced. This is a direct effect of the market economy, which has direct benefits for the development of social production and the improvement of economic situation. Some scholars who study the problem of modernization mentioned that in the traditional agricultural society, people are accustomed to planting in the spring and harvest in the fall, living depending on the gift of heaven and earth, and indulging in leisure in the slack season, thereby a lot of values related to excessive pleasure, idleness, decadence and lack of ambition are generated. Compared with this, the economic concept and economic consciousness of modern Chinese people have been much more improved. Perhaps, this is also an inner motivation behind the significant achievements that China has made with the more than 30 years of reform and opening up.

## 2. A Gentleman Fond of Wealth Will Gain It in the Proper Way

Wealth is important for life, and to some extent, it also represents the value of life in a certain aspect. Chinese people tend to divide the wealth into material wealth and spiritual wealth. Material wealth constitutes the material goods for human life and survival, including money, property, and other material resources like basic necessities; spiritual wealth includes human thought, will, faith and their spiritual value. In China, there is a proverb: A gentleman fond of wealth will gain it in the proper way. The "wealth" mentioned in this proverb is often interpreted as the material wealth represented by money in many people's view. For a long time, this proverb is regarded as a principle of survival and life that many Chinese people adhere to in their lifetime, and also the economic ethics that a lot of people abide by. It can be said that this proverb is the plainest content in the economic values of the Chinese, from which we learn that the importance is not whether or not people should pursue interests and gain wealth, but the criteria and principles for pursuing interests and gaining wealth.

In life, we can find that all ordinary people are fond of wealth and willing to get wealth, and just because they are ordinary, it is likely that their ways and means to get wealth are very common. Sometimes, if the longing for wealth become their greatest desire, they probably take a variety of methods to gain wealth, and even use improper means. However, the gentleman is different from the ordinary people; a gentleman is a man of virtue and values virtue. In terms of the wish for wealth, there's not much difference between a gentleman and an ordinary man, but they will follow different principles in gaining wealth, such principles is what we called the proper way. Then, what is the proper way and what's the use of the proper way?

Market supervision (CNSPHOTO)

> Wealth and high position are desired by all men, but if they are not gained in the right way, they should not be accepted. Poverty and low position are hated by all men, but if they cannot be rid of in the right way, they should not be given up.

Confucius said:

Wealth and high position are desired by all men, but if they are not gained in the right way, they should not be accepted. Poverty and low position are hated by all men, but if they cannot be rid of in the right way, they should not be given up. (*The Analects* • *Book 4*)

Here, the Master tells about a situation of men in the face of life, social position and wealth, and also conveys a feasible principle of conduct. The "right way" he stresses is exactly the proper way for a gentleman's gaining of wealth as we mentioned. According to Confucianism, such a proper way is etiquette, benevolence and righteousness, that is, the criterion and basis for people's gaining of wealth and obtaining of interests. All those in line with the etiquette, law, benevolence, integrity and righteousness are conforming to the proper way, and thereby reaching the basic conditions for obtaining benefits. That is to say, a gentleman can gain wealth without being condemned in accordance with this proper way. Thus, the abidance by and the implementation of the proper way becomes a virtue of gentlemen in their engaging in economic activities and gaining of wealth. Those people who are able to observe disciplines and laws and obey social etiquette and order and those people who emphasize benevolence, righteousness and integrity become the noble men who obtain interests legally. For thousands of years, such noble men and their behavior of obtaining interests are recognized by all the Chinese people; therefore, "a gentleman fond of wealth will gain it in the proper way" becomes a basic rule followed by many people when they are seeking ma-

For thousands of years, such noble men and their behavior of obtaining interests are recognized by all the Chinese people; therefore, "a gentleman fond of wealth will gain it in the proper way" becomes a basic rule followed by many people when they are seeking material interests.

terial interests.

The relationship between wealth and the proper way reflects the relationship between interests and righteousness, and the later relationship is an ethical proposition that has always been circulating in the Chinese society for thousands of years, which influences and determines people's economic values. The Confucian thought values social ethics rather than personal development; therefore more emphases are placed on righteousness than interests, thus there forms a basic value judgment that righteousness is more important than interests, righteousness has priority over interests, and righteousness is predominant over interests. Dong Zhongshu, a great Chinese scholar of Western Han Dynasty, once said something that is insightful and can be regarded as the representative of the Confucian view of righteousness and interests:

> man is born with the sense of righteousness and interests. Interests are used to nurture his body and righteousness is used to nurture his heart. He cannot feel happy in heart without righteousness and cannot feel easy in body without interests. Since righteousness is the nutrition of heart and interests are the nutrition of body; and the body is less important than the heart, righteousness is the most valuable nutrition, which is more important to man's life than interests. (*Luxuriant Dew of the Spring and Autumn Annals • Righteousness Is the Most Valuable Nutrition of Life*)

Just as what is advocated in it, although interests are also very important, they focus on man's external part, that is, human body; while righteousness focuses on man's heart, thought and spirit. Those who understand this principle will think twice and scrupulously take actions in the face of material interests and material wealth, constrain their own desire for wealth and substance in accordance with the proper way of a gentleman, and manage to bear righteousness in mind when tempted by interests, attach importance to righteousness, give weight to righteousness and make light of unrighteousness, and take righteousness as an honor and take unrighteousness as a shame.

Of course, in real life, there is also a concept that "men die for money as birds die for food" among some people. Those who hold such a concept are actually exaggerating the position of wealth especially money in life. It is objective and no problem to say that human survival and development need certain material conditions. However, it is improper to deem all the value of people's life and live to be for the purpose of obtaining money and other material wealth. In the values that support the development and progress of Chinese people for thousands of years, we cannot say the values of the pursuit of wealth are wrong; instead, what is wrong is the tendency of overstating the importance of money and other material wealth and regarding them as something sacred, extreme and one-sided. In the values of the traditional Chinese, such tendency is not obvious, and in the values of the modern Chinese, it is not dominant either. In the face of wealth, Chinese people like to judge whether or not it is ill-gotten wealth: the one in accord with moral principles is righteous wealth, that is, what a gentleman values, whereas the ill-gotten wealth is undesirable, to take ill-gotten wealth is to violate the virtue of a gentleman.

To define the appropriateness and reasonableness of people's pursuit of wealth with moral principles is a manifestation of the traditional Chinese social civilization. Why? The reason is simple, in any social system, the infinite expansion of people's desire for the pursuit of wealth, especially material wealth, will inevitably lead to the expansion of individual greed and personal desire, which will bring about the unlimited competition and demoralization and result in a social-ecological environment where people are so materialistic and blinded by greed. To take moral principles as the prerequisite for people's engaging in economic activities and obtaining of material wealth, to a certain extent, can restrict their disorderly and excessive competition, so as to build a sound economic order. Thanks to moral principles, there are more understanding, tolerance and forgiveness between people, and thereby the society will be more beautiful and progressive. An attitude towards wealth like this can be considered as a scientific and moral one. And the economic activities under the guidance of such an attitude can also to the utmost extent promote the sound development of the society.

## 3. A View of Efficiency and Fairness in the Distribution of Interests

Modern people particularly economists often illustrate the problem of the distribution of results and interests of social production with the examples of "baking a cake" and "dividing the cake". Baking a bigger and better "cake" means to make efforts to expand production, create wealth, and increase accumulation; dividing the "cake" more fairly means to distribute the wealth and interests well, avoiding various contradictions and social problems arising therefrom. In the last analysis, it is a matter of social production as to how to bake the "cake" bigger and better, whereas how to divide the "cake" more fairly is more about a matter of interest distribution. However, the distribution of interests is not as simple as who takes more "cakes" and who takes less; we still need to take into account the problem about who ought to take the "cake". Thus, the problem about the efficiency and fairness in the distribution of interests is put on the table.

The economic values that we want to discuss, in the final analysis, is people's value judgments and value choices in the process of the production, distribution, possession, exchange and consumption of interests, especially economic interests. Among them, the distribution of interests is one of the intermediate links, but it is an important link playing a role of connection, for it not only embodies the respect for working ability and dignity of the interest producers, but also foreshows how the interest occupants enjoy and consume the interests. From the way of distributing interests, we can clearly see the basic attitude of a nation or society towards economic interests.

Different times and society have different principles for the distribution of interests. From a micro perspective, it is these principles for the distribution of interests that shape people's social relations. From a macro perspective, they determine the social spirit. It is believed that in the ancient primitive society and the future communist society, people follow the principle of distribution according to need in respect of the distribution of interests, which coordinates people's interest relationship on the basis of the fundamental principle of meeting the basic human needs. However, in class society, the role and status of producers and laborers established on the basis of class relations and class status are the key factors supporting the distribution of interests. China has a long history of feudal society, in which, feudal emperors and imperial power occupants as well as the feudal landlords that serve as their class basis control the power of distributing the various interests in the society. Because they are exploiting class, they exploit the fruits of labor of the masses of working people and occupy the wealth and interests created by the masses for free. Owing to the special national and historical conditions, China had not experienced an obvious and long period of capitalism. After the end of feudalism, China soon went through the transitional period of Old Democracy and New Democracy phase and then entered into the socialist period. The most basic principle of distribution of interests in the socialist society is the distribution according to work with the participation of production factors. The distribution according to production factors and work is a mode of distribution that can reflect the value of labor and ensure the efficiency and fairness in the distribution of interests to the utmost.

China has an ancient civilization with a history of thousands of years, its people do put forward some instructive ideas about the efficiency and fairness in the distribution of interests in their long-time social life and production practice, which are worth learning, inheriting and carrying forward. In regard to the emphasis on efficiency in the distribution of interests, in the long-term feudal society, there were not the values of modern democracy and fairness, the best manifestation of the respect for the efficiency of distribution is the system of rewards and punishments for one's work, while as for the fairness in the distribution of interests, its best manifestation is the egalitarianism that is an ideal concept appealed by many people in all dynasties. There is a Chinese saying "inequality rather than want is the cause of trouble", which is to say that all parties should be taken into account in the distribution of interests and the imbalance and inequality of distribution should be avoided as far as possible. Comparatively speaking, Chinese people place more emphasis on fairness than efficiency. In the Chinese history, when many dynasties were coming to an end, there would be large-scale peasant uprisings. What those peasants opposed was rather the system of the distribution of interests that they couldn't bear anymore, especially the unfair ownership of interests practiced by the landowning class than the political system at that time.

In today's China, significant achievements in economic development has been made, material achievements continue to be accumulated, and people's life has been improved basically, but the problem of efficiency and fairness in the distribution of interests becomes prominent. Some people like to measure the distribution of interests in the Chinese society with some economic indicators, such as the Gini coefficient adopted by the developed countries, and thereby conclude that China is one of the countries with the widest gap between the rich and the poor in the world, which will eventually ruin China's development. Of course, this is a one-sided conclusion opposed by a lot of people. In fact, these economic indicators are just a reference; fundamentally speaking, in order to understand and resolve the problem of the efficiency and fairness in the distribution of interests in China's economic development, we still need to respect and take account of the national conditions and development status in China, and cannot blindly copy and mechanically apply the abstract or idealized foreign economic theories as the basis for judging the truth.

In today's China, people tend to connect the problem of the efficiency and fairness in the distribution of interests with the social system of socialism. In the minds of the masses of the people, a kind of values taking the masses as the subject has been gradually developed and formed since the founding of the PRC. In socialist society, the

Social security system benefits elders (CNSPHOTO)

people are the masters, thus China is owned by the whole Chinese people, and the wealth and interests created by the people should be shared and consumed by all the people. Deng Xiaoping once pointed out that the very essence of socialism is "the liberation and development of productive forces, the elimination of exploitation and polarization between the rich and the poor and the final achievement of common prosperity", in which the liberation and development of the productive forces is actually related to the efficiency of social production, to liberate and develop the productive forces to the greatest extent is the fundamental task of the socialist society, and meanwhile, who and how to liberate and develop the productive forces determine the problem about efficiency that must be taken into account in the distribution of interests. The elimination of exploitation and polarization between the rich and the poor and the final achievement of common prosperity is actually related to the fairness in the distribution of interests; no exploitation, no polarization and the achievement of common prosperity is exactly the largest and the most basic fairness in the socialist society.

In the past more than 30 years since the reform and opening up, the Party and the State explored the issue of social efficiency and fairness in a progressive manner, from "encouraging some people to get rich first" at the very beginning, to "taking account of both efficiency and fairness" put forward at the 14th Party Congress in 1992, and then to "efficiency is priority and fairness should also be taken into consideration" put forward after the Third Session of the 14th Party Congress in 1993, and to "more emphasis on social equity" put forward at the Fifth Session of the 16th Party Congress in 2005, people's understanding of the production, labor and creation as well as their value gradually get mature, improved, scientific and reasonable. More and more people support that in the distribution of interests, we should insist on the principle that efficiency is priority and fairness should also be taken into consideration. Such a principle is the guideline for solving the problem of distribution of interests existing in China's economic and social development at present and in the future and handling the relationships between production and possession, getting rich first and common rich, and competition and cooperation, in addition it is also an important part in the economic values of the contemporary Chinese.

## 4. A View of Civilized and Harmonious Ecological Resources

It is an indisputable fact that the Chinese nation has a long history of civilization of thousands of years. The civilization is not just in name, but in reality. In the long history of thousands of years, Chinese people created a civilized way of survival and life, in which the advocating of the harmony between man and nature and society is one of the most prominent features. Civilization and harmony is the way to wisdom and development. For civilization, if it does not comply with the law of scientific development, it will inevitably be short-lived; for harmony, if it does not take the permanent harmony as its supreme and intrinsic value pursuit, it will not last long either. Through a comparison between the history of Chinese and Western civilization, we can draw an obvious conclusion: it is precisely in the pursuit of civilization and harmony that the Chinese history can shine with dazzling brilliance and the Chinese people are able to achieve considerable development and progress.

Since ancient times, there has been a kind of pragmatic economic values in the minds of the Chinese people. The ancient Chinese people believed that man is the master of nature, and all kinds of objective resources in the natural world can be developed and utilized by man, thus benefiting mankind and realizing their value. However, in such a view that advocates managing and utilizing resources and objects in the outside world, the development and utilization is not savage or unrestricted but temperate and limited. In modern words, Chinese people have formed a kind of economic values of scientifically treating nature and moderately utilizing resources long ago. Such economic values can be illustrated with the Chinese classic maxims: as early as the Spring and Autumn Period, in order to protect nature and prevent man's destruction of nature through overexploitation and deforestation, Confucius proposed "fishing without using a net; shooting without aiming at birds perching" (*The Analects* • *Book 7*); Mencius also proposed that do not "fish by emptying the water of a pond", "the seasons of husbandry should not be interfered with", "close nets are not allowed to enter the pools and ponds" and "the axes and bills enter the hills and forests only at the proper time" (*Mencius • King Hui of Liang* Ⅰ); Xunzi stressed to "strengthen agricultural production and economize expenses", "make provisions sufficient and go into production at the proper season" (*Xunzi • Discussion of Heaven*). All these arguments, such as not catching all in one net when fishing and forbidding deforestation when lumbering, are for the purpose of the economy and regeneration of resources. It should be acknowledged that such a view of resource utilization in favor of going into production in line with seasons and laws and forbidding overexploitation advocated by the ancient Chinese is civilized, scientific and reasonable, which is also beneficial to the development of mankind itself and the natural world.

Glaciers melting in the Alps

The view advocated by the ancient Chinese on the protection of nature as well as the reasonable development and moderate utilization of resources contains a kind of civilized, harmonious and dialectical economic values. All things in the world, including humans, are supplementing, promoting and restricting each other, and there is a relationship of mutually connecting, constraining and being constrained among them. Many Chinese people believe human being's exploitation of natural resources has limits, and if people's economic activities simply evolve into a profit-seeking activity of exploiting natural resources in a savage and unrestricted manner, then the interests of human beings will eventually be harmed. Therefore, our ancestors wisely proposed the view of developing and utilizing resources in an economical, timely and moderate way, which embodies the civilized and harmonious values. The seasons of husbandry should not be interfered with, the natural resources should not be wasted, the development and utilization of resources should be economical, and the resources should be developed and utilized in the proper way. Aren't all these the manifestations of civilization? Aren't they the manifestations of the pursuit of harmonious coexistence between heaven, earth, man and all things? The economic values reflected in such a view show it is not true that the ancients did not attach importance to the economic value of resources and materials; on the contrary, they were clearly aware of the limit and essence of their economic value.

In the course of modernization of the world, many developed countries of today have tried to achieve modernization by means of industrialization and commercialization. In their process of economic development, there were wanton exploitation of resources as well as pollution and destruction of ecological environment in various degrees. Later, when they became aware of the importance of the protection of ecological resources and environment, they turned to take remedial measures, attempting to develop ecological civilization.

Looking back on it now, the development road of "pollution first, treatment later" and "destruction first, protection later" taken by the Western developed countries is just like locking the stable door after the horse has been stolen, which is a lesson to the developing China and Chinese people. On the basis of fully drawing development experience and lessons of all countries and all times and proceeding from the reality of national conditions, the Party and the Government of China put forward the scientific outlook on development. The scientific outlook on development is an important idea guiding China's economic and social development, as well as a guideline for the realization of the civilized and harmonious utilization of ecological resources in the present era, which takes putting people first as its core, comprehensive, balanced and sustainable development as its goal, and overall consideration as its fundamental approach. Since the 17th Congress of CPC in 2007, to attach importance to the scientific use of ecological resources and enhance energy conservation and environmental protection has become a basic national policy that Chinese people firmly believe and sincerely carry out. In addition, to build a resource-saving and environment-friendly society and improve the capacity for sustainable development has also become an important administrative principle for all kinds of departments at all levels. The consciousness of ecological civilization, the awareness of resources and environment, and the realization of the harmonious development and friendly coexistence between heaven, earth, man and things have been already rooted in people's minds, becoming the important values in their engaging in social production and economic life.

# Chapter Five

# The Diverse and Inclusive Cultural Values

# 5

# The Diverse and Inclusive Cultural Values

> Every form of beauty has its uniqueness. Precious is to appreciate other forms of beauty with openness. If beauty represents itself with diversity and integrity, the world will be blessed with harmony and beauty.

Chinese culture has a long and profound history and enjoys great prestige in the world, the civilization of ancient China would make people feel a sense of yearning and reverence, and in the modern times it is still glamorous and attractive enough to catch the eyes of the whole world. Chinese culture is the culture of the Chinese people, which is created and enjoyed by them. The reason why Chinese culture is able to remain fresh for thousands of years and have tremendous attraction and cohesion is related to the cultural values of respecting and tolerating diversity upheld by the Chinese people as well as the tolerant ethos and broad-minded spirit inside the Chinese culture. Chinese sociologist Fei Xiaotong once proposed a cultural view, called "The Four Lines of Beauty": "Every form of beauty has its uniqueness. Precious is to appreciate other forms of beauty with openness. If beauty represents itself with diversity and integrity, the world will be blessed with harmony and beauty". These words are not only the description of the intrinsic quality of the traditional Chinese cultural values, but also the expectation of the cultural exchanges and coexistence between different nations and countries as well as the development of human culture under the conditions of globalization. From these four lines, we can clearly see the diverse and inclusive values in respect of culture upheld by the Chinese people.

## 1. A View of Harmonious But not Uniform Cultural Relations

It is often said that values are the core of the culture. The culture mentioned here is the one in the broad sense, which refers to the all-inclusive "macro culture", including both the material creation and spiritual accumulation. The culture in the narrow sense only refers to the spiritual cultural achievements created by man, specifically referring to the cultural products such as thought, literature, art and religion. Culture is not only originated from different groups of cultural creation, but also able to be shared among different groups; it can not only exist within one country, but also transcend national boundaries, existing in different countries. When different cultures constitute the cultural units or cultural genres with different nature, content, and elements, the problems about what the relationships are between them and how the different cultures get along with each other are involved with the cultural values.

Culture is the spiritual product of people's activities, therefore, the cultural relations are actually also the reflection of the relations of people's activities in respect of ideological value judgment and spiritual value pursuit formed in the history. Since a very early time, people have had a wish to observe and analyze the culture life and cultural ethos of different nations, different societies and groups; until today, people are still always discussing and comparing different types of culture, and they even have upgraded such a discussion and comparison to the science of cultural relations. In the 1940s, Chen Xujing, a scholar of Chinese culture, wrote a book *A General Survey of Cul-*

*turology*. This book discusses the cultural phenomenon and the cultural view, in which the most vivid content is the part that is involved with the discussion of several relations in the cultural development, including the relations between the inheritance and development of culture, the freedom and equality between cultures, the harmony and conflict between cultures, and so on.

As for the comparison of cultural relations, in general, there are two types. One is the comparison within a country, or in other words, within a certain big culture. The Chinese culture that we usually say is a general title, which is the generalization of the cultures of all areas, all ethnic groups and all regions in China. Within the Chinese culture, there are of course various local and categorized cultures, in which the former includes culture of the Yellow River, culture of the Yangtze River, Northern culture, Southern culture, Southwest culture and cultures of other areas, the latter includes wine culture, tea culture, festival culture, food culture, dress culture and a variety of cultures of other categories. If we conduct a comparative study between the culture of the Yellow River and the culture of the Yangtze River or between the Northern culture and the Southern culture, we will be able to find out the cultural relations between different regions within the Chinese culture. And similarly, if we make a comparison between the cultures of different categories, then we can see the cultural relations between them. The other is the comparison between different countries, or rather, between the cultures of some specific countries or societies. In the modern society, those works entitled "Comparison of Chinese and Western Culture", "Comparison of Chinese and Western Art" or something like this actually contain the comparisons of the cultural relations between different countries, societies, nations and races.

Although people can generalize cultural relations from many different perspectives, in brief, there are no more than two categories of relations between cultures, namely, conflict and harmony. In the history of human culture, there are some expansionary cultures (or cultures that have prominent expansionary nature in certain development phases). In their development process, they always conflict with and harass other cultures, or even try to invade and annihilate others. Such terms as cultural colonialism, cultural imperialism and cultural hegemony are the description of the nature or fundamental stance of this kind of cultures. Dominated by such nature or stance of culture, some countries take it for granted that their own cultural values formed in their history are the universal values and intend to carry out them in cultures of other nations in the world by force, making other nations and countries also believe in their values, thus when meeting with difficulties and resistance, they can attack or intervene by the use of economic, political and military force without the slightest scruple. Obviously, the cultural relations under the domination of such ideology can never be harmonious, but often antagonistic, conflicting and intense.

There is still a kind of culture that is smooth and inclusive, and always in the pursuit of harmony and integration between different cultures. In the day-to-day development of the culture, especially at the time when a culture meets with another heterogeneous culture, this kind of culture will not try to invade or annihilate the other one, but proceed from peaceful values and reasonably integrate with the heterogeneous culture, attempt to absorb its excellent content and

> Chinese culture belongs to the type that pursues the harmonious cultural relations.

remove the impact of its inferior content. Chinese culture belongs to the type that pursues the harmonious cultural relations. Although in the history of China, it is inevitable that the integration of Chinese culture was accompanied by local and temporary conflicts, all these conflicts occurred within the Chinese nation, and they were not fundamental and decisive cultural conflicts. From the political and military point of view, any nation and country with a long history has records of war, China is no exception. However, from the point of view of cultural relations, a distinct character of Chinese culture different from Western culture is that it takes the pursuit of harmony, integration and coexistence as its mainstream values.

Prayers for the country and people by monks in front of the Longmen Grottoes

Since the ancient times, the Chinese people have always advocated peace, loathed war, avoided conflict, and refused to show off, instead, they would like to make concessions to avoid trouble. Whenever it comes to cultural issues, Chinese people will naturally think of "harmony without uniformity" and "harmony is prized", and those Western scholars who have an in-depth understanding of the Chinese people and the Chinese culture also perceive Chinese people's character of advocating harmony, some of whom sincerely admit that Chinese people have a peaceful heart. In the previous part, we have cited the example of the British philosopher Bertrand Russell; in fact, there are a lot of Westerners who hold the same standpoint with Russell before or after him. They all believe that the Chinese culture is a culture advocating harmony but not uniformity, a culture not only developing itself but also allowing others' development. Behind such culture, it is the view of harmonious but not uniform cultural relations pursued by the Chinese people. And behind such view of cultural relations, it is the wisdom and experience possessed and treasured by the Chinese people and the Chinese culture, that is, respecting other cultures and recognizing the diversity, pluralism, specificities, and complexity of culture.

In the present era, culture is spreading around the world. Compared with the past, the culture of a nation can influence another nation in a faster, bigger and stronger way by means of modern science and technology. This, on the one hand, is the charm of cultural globalization, on the other hand, is also the cause of the conflicts and disputes between nations or countries with different types of culture. For any kind of culture, when it is confronted with other cultures, if it always tries to prevail over all the others, holds a hostile attitude towards them, or simply annihilates them, then the world we are living in will never be in peace and mankind will never be happy. Just as what Alpha Oumar Konaré, the former President of Mali, said, "as long as any civilization applies political, intellectual and moral coercion on others on the basis of the endowments nature and history have bequeathed to it, there can be no hope of peace for humanity: the negation of the cultural specificities of any people is tantamount to the negation of its dignity".

## 2. A View of Incongruous and Diverse Cultural Beliefs

Speaking of cultural values, we have to talk about the problem of beliefs. The belief is a mental problem, as well as a social and cultural problem. What are the beliefs of the Chinese people? This still seems to be a very complex question so far, or a mystery that is too difficult to solve. As regards the beliefs of the Chinese people, not only foreigners feel confused, but even Chinese people themselves also feel difficult to make it clear in a short while. There is a widely circulated story about the cultural beliefs of Chinese people. It goes like this: Confucius, Laozi and Buddha, who are the representatives of Confucianism, Taoism and Buddhism respectively, one day came across in the land of the Immortals, and they all lamented the decadence of the mortal world, therefore they decided to look for a model who is able to put their doctrines into practice, thus guiding the people in the world. After searching for some time, Confucius met a highly respected elder who was extremely familiar with his doctrine, but when Confucius took his leave, the elder did not rise to see him off. Then Confucius recommended Laozi and Buddha to visit this sitting philosopher. As a result, both Laozi and Buddha found the elder to be also very versed in their doctrines, and a model of eloquence and fervor, but he did not rise from his seat. These three founders of religion believed that the elder was the very one who is able to pass on the three religions and realize the "unity of the three religions" well. When they came before the elder and stated their intentions, the elder said: "I do know your doctrines and even I'm quite familiar with some of the content. However, it is only from my waist upward that I am a man, below that I am made of stone; I hold firm belief in all your doctrines, but I can never put any of them into practice." We can explain the meaning of this story from different perspective. However, it can be concluded that Chinese people's beliefs are complex.

Arthur H. Smith who is an American missionary of 19th century and has an in-depth understanding of the Chinese people since the modern times, his *Chinese Characteristics* not only received high praise from Gu Hongming, Lin Yutang and Lu Xun, but also greatly influenced foreigners' perception of the Chinese people and the Chinese culture. In this book, he specially uses a chapter "Multi-beliefs" to describe the spiritual pursuit and cultural values of the Chinese people. He also cited the above story to illustrate the state of the cultural beliefs of the Chinese people. In his opinion, the classic Confucianism may be the doctrine that to the greatest extent affect and shape the beliefs of the Chinese people. In addition to this, it seems that none of the belief in God, hero worship, nature worship and idol worship can reach an agreement among the majority of the Chinese people. Thus, he concluded that there is very little which one can be safe in predicating of the Chinese Empire as a whole. It seems that the pure atheism prevails in the upper classes of Chinese society, while polytheism and pantheism are popular among the common people in the lower class. Smith's point of view is not alone in the cognitive world of Westerners, a lot of Westerners and even many Chinese people are also holding the same view on the cultural beliefs of the Chinese. The reasonableness of such a view is that it accurately points out the incongruity and diversity of the cultural beliefs in the values of the Chinese.

Throughout the history, there have been always some people exploring the cultural beliefs or spiritual beliefs of the Chinese and trying to use a kind of fixed object to denote their beliefs, but unfortunately, they all failed, because they always judge the beliefs of the Chinese from a one-dimensional perspective and observe their spiritual world with one eye, thus inevitably drawing one-sided conclusions. In fact, Chinese people's beliefs are incongruous, diverse and complex, which is difficult to be denoted and covered by one single belief. For China always has the largest population in the world, it is really unrealistic and almost impossible to find out a uniform and fixed object of belief for so many Chinese people.

The reason why the cultural beliefs of the Chinese are incongruous and diverse is certainly related to the large population, varied social class structure and complex social order and system of China, meanwhile, it is also concerned with the fact that Chinese people live in the vast land and their local cultures have miscellaneous and diverse origins. In China, different groups of people are engaged in different social production in different regions, and there are differences in their way of life and accumulation of culture, therefore, people from different places hold different beliefs. Within the vast territory, southerners and northerners have different beliefs, and there are differences in beliefs between people living in the east and people living in the west; this is incredible in a small country, but in China, it is very common. Even in the same region, the people with different status, roles and occupations also have different beliefs. Therefore, looking back into the history of China, we can find that one of the most obvious features is that all classes including the monarch, the nobility, officials, ordinary people, as well as scholars, farmers, artisans and merchants have their own cultural sentiments and survival beliefs.

Owing to the profoundness, broadness, generosity and inclusiveness of Chinese culture, all different cultural beliefs are able to tolerate the others' existence and development and coexist in peace and harmony. This not only reflects the greatness of Chinese culture, but also represents the foundation for the great cultural achievements in China. Towards the same cultural belief, Chinese people do not like the Westerners who firmly believe in a single religion, and even if they believe in a religion with great passion, they will not detach themselves from reality or immerse themselves in religious life. Xia Mianzun said, "can not believe in it too much, and cannot believe in it too less, this is the attitude of the Chinese people towards beliefs!" (*The Coexistence and Moderation*), and the old saying "rather believe that it exists

Owing to the profoundness, broadness, generosity and inclusiveness of Chinese culture, all different cultural beliefs are able to tolerate the others' existence and development and coexist in peace and harmony.

than not; rather believe it to be truth than not" is the principle for beliefs of the majority of the Chinese people, which precisely reflects the Chinese people's cultural attitude of believing in but not indulging in.

Different from Westerners, Chinese people can believe in different gods, different Buddhas and different regions follow their own bent and as their own wishes. Cultural beliefs, in the eyes of many Westerners, are a powerful force. The belief in a certain kind of cultural idol, regardless of Jesus Christ or Allah, can always generate a sense of devotion and awe in people's minds, and because there are beliefs, people can have fear and thus have pursuit and restraint. In the eyes of Chinese people, cultural beliefs are also a powerful force, but this force is not imposed by the outside world or foreign objects, but from the willingness and consciousness in the bottom of their hearts. Therefore, the cultural idols that Chinese people believe in will not bring them the sense of awe and oppression, and Chinese people are holding a deferential, reverent and almost sacred attitude towards the idols in their cultural beliefs.

In the religious policy of contemporary China, each person enjoys full freedom of religious belief. As long as he does not believe in evil cults or use them to endanger the security of the state and the society as well as the well-being of the people, people can choose to and refuse to believe in any religion, and the right to be a believer or non-believer is in their own hands. In China's political ideology and cultural thought, each person also enjoys full political freedom and cultural rights, as long as he does not deliberately harm the security of the state and the society as well as the well-being of the people. Thus, the differences of the cultural values of people are fully respected and the diversity of their ideological concepts is accepted to the greatest extent.

## 3. A View of Cultural Utilization Through Learning from Others

There is a Chinese proverb "An inch has its length and a foot sometimes falls short", which means everything has its advantages and weaknesses, and only through supplementing each other can different things coexist. This proverb is able to reflect the cultural values of the Chinese, in which the core is the view of cultural utilization, that is, local Chinese culture's learning from other cultures. As a matter of fact, like any other nation in the world, Chinese people cherish their cultural tradition very much and have full confidence in the future of their culture. In addition, there is another distinct characteristic in the cultural values of the Chinese, that is, they attach much importance to the value and significance of other cultures, and thereby develop a habit of being good at examining and accepting good opinions and learning from and making use of the advantages in other cultures.

Confucius said: "When I walk along with two others, they may serve me as my teachers. I will select their good qualities and follow them, their bad qualities and avoid them." (*The Analects* · *Book 7*) And in the *Three*

> When I walk along with two others, they may serve me as my teachers. I will select their good qualities and follow them, their bad qualities and avoid them.

*Character Primer* that is the most popular moral book in China, it mentions: "Of old, Confucius took Hsiang T'o for his teacher", which is about the story that Confucius learnt from Hsiang T'o who is a child prodigy. Even to this day, many people still take delight in the story that Confucius learnt from a little boy. From the words and deeds of Confucius, we can see that it contains a kind of view of learning that advocates learning from others' advantages to make up for one's own weaknesses recognized by the Chinese nation, what's more, it also embodies a cultural value judgment of being good at learning and making progress. In fact, if we take a look at the process of the creation, accumulation, and formation of the Chinese culture, we will be able to have a more profound understanding of Chinese people's view of cultural utilization through learning from others.

The main body of the Chinese culture is the Huaxia culture, which is, Han culture; the Han nationality itself is formed through the integration of many ethnic groups, and Han culture itself is also the integration of a variety of cultures. In the early period when the Han nationality was just formed, those non-Han aboriginal tribes or minority nationalities also had their own cultures, however, their cultures were absorbed and utilized into the unified Huaxia culture in the process of national integration. In Chinese history, there appeared several times of regime disruption and national integration, and such times were exactly the periods in which cultural exchanges were unprecedentedly active and national association was more frequent. For example, during the Southern and Northern Dynasties period, there was an event called the "Wu Hu Uprising", which actually refers to the cultural integration between Han and minorities. During that period, Persian in the West, Xianbei, Qiang, Di in the North, Miao,

Li in the South and other tribes or minority nationalities all flooded into Zhong Yuan (the Central Plains of China) and integrated with each other there, people of Hu (northern non-Chinese nomadic tribes) gradually accepted the culture and customs of Han people and merged into Han; and Han also absorbed their merits and advantages and used them in their own life.

The Tang Dynasty of China is another period in which Chinese people's view of cultural utilization through learning from others can be fully reflected. Generally speaking, the prosperity and the open atmosphere of the Tang Dynasty are highly praised by all, especially the Reign of Zhenguan under the rule of Emperor Taizong of Tang and the Heyday of Kaiyuan under the reign of Emperor Xuanzong of Tang. At that time, Zhong Yuan culture accepted and absorbed many foreign cultures, which include not only the cultures within the Chinese territory, but also those cultures from foreign cultures with more distinct differences. An obvious example is that at that time, Buddhism, Christianity and Islam were spreading and existing simultaneously in China, and all these religions are not originated from China. In addition, at the time of giving and contributing a large number of outstanding cultural achievements to the people of the world, Tang Dynasty was also absorbing and taking advantage of the cultural achievements from foreign nations and lands.

The reason why we take the Tang Dynasty as an example is that it is the most typical and representative dynasty that can reflect that Chinese people and Chinese culture are good at absorbing and learning from exotic cultures, but this did not in the least affect and belittle the Chinese culture's absorption and learning from exotic cultures in other dynasties in the process of cultural exchanges between China and foreign countries. Besides the flourishing Han and Tang dynasties, in the periods of Song, Yuan, Ming and Qing dynasties, Chinese people's view of opening up became wider rather than narrowing, and also the cultural exchanges between China and foreign countries had new expansion in respect of area and content. In the existing documents about Sino-foreign cultural exchanges that can be consulted, especially those historical material written and left by foreigners, we can find a lot of examples of this aspect.

Emperor Taizong of Tang

The view of cultural utilization through learning from others is in a macro sense of the Chinese culture. In a more specific sense, that is, in the aspect of the Chinese people themselves as well as their daily life, such cultural values of being good at learning from others' advantages to make up for their own weaknesses not only fit in with the moral character of reforming and improving themselves, being modest and studious, and striving for progress and innovation of the Chinese people, but also are in line with the moral standard of stressing self-warning, self-examination, self-consciousness and self-motivation in the Chinese culture. In traditional Chinese society, when gentlemen or scholars cultivated their own moral character, they tended to follow the principle of "learning from others' advantages to make up for one's own weaknesses" and the saying that "When we see men of worth, we should think of equaling them; when we see men of a contrary character, we should turn inwards and examine ourselves". What they excelled at and advocated most was the self-examination, through which, they were able to find out their own weaknesses and mistakes in thought and behavior, and thus make efforts to correct them.

Zengzi

The cultural value judgment expressed by the principle of learning from others' advantages to make up for one's own weaknesses is that although one's own culture is worth cherishing, it is not always perfect; while although others' culture is not perfect either, it always has saving grace. Such a cultural value judgment fully embodies the thinking model of "putting oneself in another's place" and the value choice of "laying equal stress on self-respect and respect for others" in the Chinese culture. Culture is something deep-seated and with profound influence. The view of learning from others in the Chinese people's cultural concept is beneficial not only to ensuring the Chinese culture to be always in a state of learning and progressing, but also to supporting the Chinese people in keeping their spiritual orientation modest and prudent and free from arrogance and rashness in the economic and social life, and thereby maintains the progress of both the Chinese people and the Chinese culture and civilization.

## 4. A View of Harmonious, Happy and Shared Cultural Home

"If the family lives in harmony, all affairs will prosper". Traditional Chinese society advocates the idea that "the world is a family", in which people complies with a special concept and order of "family". Chinese people attach importance to the family and more importance to the harmony of the family, because they believe that only home is the haven that make people feel happiest and most serene, and only a harmonious family can support the property of its members' undertakings. For thousands of years, the Chinese nation has worked together to create a big family, that is, the Great China. In this family, the members have always been creating and enjoying the brilliant Chinese civilization and Chinese culture. Despite the differences in ethnic group, language, region, food, clothing and other habits, Chinese people share the common cultural gene and common cultural attribution, that is, the extremely comprehensive and inclusive Chinese culture as well as its inner spirit. In terms of both tone and nature, Chinese culture is the summation of cultures of all ethnic groups living in the land of China; therefore, the inner spirit and values of the Chinese culture is unified and integrated. Regardless of the numerous micro-cultural differences, the common Chinese culture ties the hearts of hundreds of millions of Chinese people together tightly.

According to archaeological research, the origin of the Chinese family appeared about at the end of the primitive society and the beginning of the slave-owning society. At that time, along with the emergence of private ownership and the progress of social production, the family with the spouse system and property system at its core came into being. Through thousands of years, the concept of family is deeply rooted in the hearts of the Chinese people, and the values born and existing in the family are also intertwined in their minds like a continuous chain. Different from the home in the material sense, the Chinese nation's concept of home in the cultural sense has a long process of gestation. In this process, of course, there are some contradictions and conflicts between different ethnic groups and different social classes, but in the concept of the Chinese people and in the Chinese culture, "harmony" is the mainstream, "happiness" is the supreme pursuit, and the cultural home is the place where all the Chinese people and all the members of the Chinese nation will finally settle.

After the Qin and Han dynasties, since the feudal regime in China carried out the policy of Confucianism worship, the Confucian doctrine was upgraded to the dominant political and social ideology. Although the values advocated by Confucianism underwent some changes in the two thousand years thereafter, its core values have never changed. Such Confucian core values have not only turned into the kernel of the Chinese culture, but also been deeply rooted in the hearts of the Chinese people, becoming the backbone of their world of value as well as the basic content that shapes and constitutes their view of cultural home. Until today, a lot of Chinese people still preserve the traditional Confucian values in their words and deeds and follow the requirements of spiritual values of the Chinese culture.

Tung Chung-shu

> Almost in every dynasty in the Chinese history, there was integration between ethnic groups in marginal areas and in the central plains of China, between Han and minorities.

When it comes to the cultural home of the Chinese, we cannot fail to mention the great national integration. China is a unified multi-ethnic country, however, the national unity and integration is not formed at the very beginning, but in the long-term historical development process.

Almost in every dynasty in the Chinese history, there was integration between ethnic groups in marginal areas and in the central plains of China, between Han and minorities; from the pre-Qin to the Ming and Qing Dynasties, the degree of national integration might be higher or lower, but the course of integration had almost never been interrupted. The great national integration is also the great cultural integration, the Chinese nation and the Chinese culture are formed in the integration, and the view of cultural home of the Chinese is also shaped in the integration.

In Chinese history, there are many great emperors and heroes, who made significant contributions to the integration of Chinese nation and the unification of China with their outstanding cultural and military achievements. The Emperor Qin Shihuang, Emperor Wudi of Han, Emperor Taizong of Tang and Emperor Taizu of Song mentioned in Mao Zedong's poem are the emperors who made contributions to the unification of China in different periods, whereas Qi Jiguang, Zheng Chenggong, Lin Zexu and Zuo Zongtang are the heroes who fought against foreign invaders and made contributions to the prevention of the split of the nation and the state in different dynasties. Nevertheless, those who play a real leading role in the unification and integration of the Chinese nation are the most ordinary but greatest masses of people, for they represent the real motive power of historical development as well as the powerful force that determines the direction of history. It is the participation and involvement of the people that ultimately shape the Chinese nation's cultural values that advocate a harmonious, happy and united home.

Since Chinese people have a unified and shared cultural home, they naturally have a common national spirit and a common spiritual

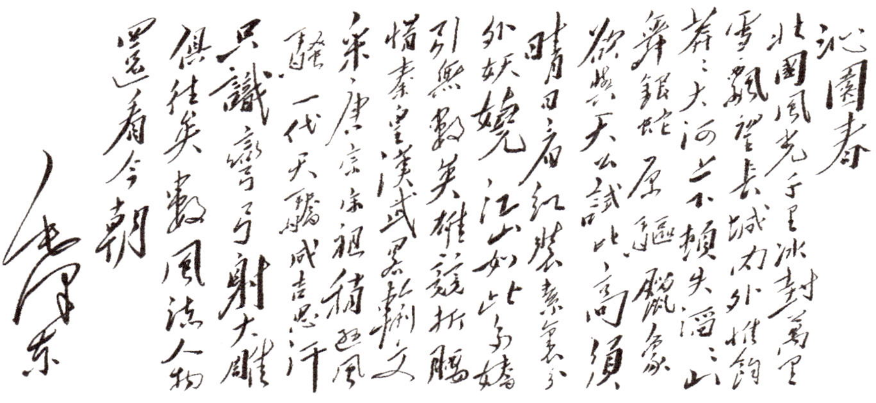

*Snow—to the Tune of Chin Yuan Chun*, by Mao Zedong

home. Such a spiritual home is more solid and perdurable than the mountains and rivers and more worth making all efforts and sacrificing everything to defend. During the thousands of years, in their common practice of production and life, the Chinese people have gradually formed a national spirit of solidarity, unity, industry, bravery, loving peace and keeping progress that takes the patriotism as its core. Among them, the deep-level spiritual requirement of patriotism is to love the cultural home shared by the Chinese people. The regimes and dynasties in Chinese history have gone forever with their changes, however the Chinese culture survives and accumulates thicker and thicker, stronger and stronger. Any rise and fall in the history and in the world cannot eliminate the Chinese culture as well as its influence on the Chinese people.

The world today is a globalized world, in which a lot of original cultures and civilizations suffer the impact of alien cultures. In the face of globalization, many original regional cultures have been uprooted or assimilated. Towards the future, the policy of reform and opening up in China will not change; neither will the trend that China and its people get integrated into the world. In this case, the Chinese people's value pursuit of maintaining a harmonious, happy and united cultural home will inevitably meet challenges from all sides. As for how to ensure that the Chinese people always have their own cultural home, it is a problem raised by the development of the times which needs to be answered by the contemporary Chinese people.

Chapter Six

# The Civilized and Progressive Social Values

# 6 The Civilized and Progressive Social Values

People living in a certain society will always hold a variety of views on the society itself. What the social values indicate is the overall value judgments of the society made by a certain group of people, or their value pursuit manifested in the problem of social situation and social development, that is, the mental state and value goal shown by all members of the society. Thus, what the Chinese people's overall value judgments of China's social development express is exactly the social values of the Chinese.

## 1. A View of Social Collective of Respecting Work and Being Gregarious

Although there is a lot of controversy, the majority of the Chinese people, especially the intelligentsia, recognize that Chinese society is a collective-type social structure. Well, what are the sources of the Chinese people's view of valuing collective? It is generally believed that the view of collective held by the Chinese is developed in the process of the unification of China in the history, grounded on the principle of order espoused by them, rooted in the family pattern implemented by them and subject to the production situation of the Chinese society. Due to the existence of the family pattern as well as the constraint and requirement of the level of social productive forces, Chinese society stresses the social order, the status and position of people, and the role of people in the society. This is the case in contemporary China and more the case in traditional Chinese society.

Under the influence of the traditional culture, each person has his own role in the society. The whole society is a huge machine that never stops working and each person is a little screw of it. The operation of the social machine requires each person to play his own proper role in his own position. Even at home, at work and even at the place of leisure and entertainment, he still cannot break away from his own role. Since ancient times, the collective concept play a role of adhesive for various social groups in the Chinese society. Although there are contradictions and conflicts or even fierce class struggle between different members of society, the influence brought by the society as a huge collective organization still cannot be concealed or offset.

The collective concept advocated by traditional Chinese society, in essence, is a doctrine of social supremacy. In modern words, such a doctrine of social supremacy advocates altruism and rationalism, which requires that the members of society always put social and collective interests in the first place, and when their personal interests conflict with the social or collective interests, they should repress or even sacrifice the former. In the feudal society, the largest collective is the ordinary people, but the paramount collective is Heaven. The emperor as the Son of Heaven is the representative of Heaven and thus has the power of controlling and managing the collective. The collective is greater than the individual, and imperial power is higher than human rights, therefore the society becomes a patriarchal autocratic society.

Hegel said that tradition is just like a chain, a concept in the past will still appear in the modern times. Naturally, the Chinese people's view of valuing collective in the history will not disappear in contemporary Chinese people, but will be passed down and developed. In the a hundred years after the end of the feudal society, Chinese society has undergone great unrest; the occurrence of revolution on the one hand shook the traditional collective consciousness that remains in people's minds, on the other hand appealed for the organized and orderly behavior and values. In the process of revolution, construction and reform under the leadership of the Communist Party of China, new social value genes have been injected into the Chinese people's view of collective: collective is a community in which all men are equal and free; it means democracy rather than autocracy; each individual is an integral part of it, and if there is no individual, there will be no collective. It can be said that after the reform and opening up, the collective concept in the minds of contemporary Chinese people has been greatly different from that in the past, and their social collective consciousness has been renewed.

Objectively speaking, compared to the past, the view of social collective of the contemporary Chinese people has been greatly weakened. The reasons for this are mainly related to the social changes in contemporary China. The change in the traditional family structure, the individual-oriented creation and distribution of interests, and especially the influence of numerous foreign cultures in the modern trend of globalization, modernization and informatization all have changed the values of social collective of the Chinese. It has been proven by research that the view of collective of the contemporary Chinese is generally weaker than that in the past, people pay less attention to and show less consideration for the collective, and many people's consciousness of collective value and concept of collective service also become vague. It is not true to say that the Chinese people's view of society and collective has not changed since the reform and opening up, however, it seems over-exaggerated to say that such change has reached a degree where the consciousness of collective and society has been lost.

In fact, the situation is not that depressing and pessimistic. In the spring and summer of 2012, a well-known website launched a ballot to ask people's views on the contemporary Chinese society. Many voters expressed their points of view on the current situation and future trends of the social development in China. Lots of people proposed a variety of social issues, and some expressed their dissatisfaction with the status quo of the society, but the final statistics on the opinions show that more than 78% of the total number of people hold a positive view on the status quo of contemporary Chinese society, and the vast majority of Chinese people are full of confidence in China's future development and have high expectations of the bright future of the Chinese society. What is in particular gratifying is that no matter what they do for a living, Chinese people will generally be obedient to and feel satisfied with the collective where they are living, and able to gain a sense of stability and accomplishment. From the their vote on the social conditions in China, we can see the social collective values of respecting work and being gregarious of the contemporary Chinese people.

Chinese people believe that people cannot survive without working and cannot feel happy without other's company; respecting work and being gregarious is a virtue, as well as a survival skill. People can achieve success in their careers with the help of respecting work and can obtain a happy life with the help of being gregarious. In everyday life, we often hear that the parents advise their children who are going to start a career or enter

Chinese people believe that people cannot survive without working and cannot feel happy without other's company.

the society: "Do a good job" and "Get on well with others". "Do a good job" is another way of saying respecting work; and "Get on well with others" is another way to express being gregarious. What the parents' advice conveys is exactly a kind of expectation of their children's quality and capacity of respecting work and being gregarious. Such an expectation is common and realistic among the Chinese people.

Since the "iron rice bowl" (secure employment) has been broken, the contemporary Chinese people have lost the sense of belonging to the organization and unit like in the past society, but no matter how society changes, the Chinese people do not lose hope for their occupations and careers, neither do they lose their consciousness of responsibility of starting careers and making achievements. In the modern times, respecting work is still one of the professional ethics of the Chinese people, and being gregarious is still their life pursuit. From the view of respecting work and being gregarious that most people are still holding, we still can see Chinese people's love and reverence for the collective as well as their belief in and sincere practice of the collectivistic values.

## 2. A View of Free and Equal Social Democracy

Freedom and equality is the desire of human beings shown at the time of judging their own value after the modern enlightenment, and it is also the purport of the concept of democracy. Whether in the classical Western society or the ancient Chinese society, the concept of democracy including freedom and equality, in fact, is subject to the limitations of the social system in the ancient times and thus difficult to realize and exist objectively. Even if some of the sage and the wise are able to be aware of its important value, it is still just a beautiful hope. Therefore, when it comes to the values of freedom, equality and democracy, both Chinese and foreign countries are linked with the modern society, modern system and modern consciousness.

Although traditional Chinese society is an authoritarian society, modern Chinese people is no stranger to the view of free and equal social democracy. The modern democratic revolution started at the beginning of the twentieth century opened up the process of social democratization in China. Among the pioneers of the early democratic revolution in China, a lot of people came to realize the importance of the values of free and equal social democracy. Sun Yat-sen is one of the most important guides. He was actively advocating the concept of freedom and equality at that time and combined them with the opposition to autocracy as well as the establishment of democracy. He said:

> My Country is so vast in territory, so large in population and so rich in resources, how could it be so poor like this! The actual reason is that under the autocratic regime of the Qing Dynasty, the people have no right and thus have no obligation. They enjoy the happiness without freedom and equality, willingly abandon their responsibilities, and have neither competitive nor enterprising spirit. This is a major cause of the poverty and weakness of the nation.[1]

he also said:

> human beings in today's world have reached the stage of childhood of human evolution, so the idea of freedom and equality has increasingly developed, as it is called, the trend of the world cannot be reversed.[2]

Although the democratic revolution led by Sun Yat-sen failed, it brought a preliminary concept of democracy to the Chinese people. What followed was the vigorous and continuous democratic revolution.

However, the Chinese society, after all, is different from the Western society. Western-style democracy has its specific condition of existence and environment of growth; therefore, the tide of democratization in modern China did not bear the fruit as the Westerners and early Chinese democrats expected. The Communist Party of China is a great and wise political party, who earnestly grasped the national conditions in China, led the Chinese revolution, construction and reform, and started the course of building a new democracy, that is, the people's democracy and socialist democracy, by going through the new democratic revolution and the socialist revolution. Up till now, the Chinese people are still building their own democratic society with great efforts and courage.

Sun Yat-sen

In a long period of time, there is a prevailing opinion in domestic and international academic and ideological circles, which puts that China has thousands of years of feudal autocratic tradition, thus Chinese people are accustomed to the life in the feudal order and hierarchy, and they have little concepts of freedom, equality and democracy. This opinion seems logical, but in fact, its reason is insufficient. Chinese people do not have the Westerners' so-called concepts of freedom, equality and democracy, but this does not mean that they do not have the similar value pursuit of their own. Since ancient times, Chinese people's longing to get rid of the shackle between man and things, pursuit of their own liberation, and understanding of man as the master of nature and himself have been always there and never been cut off in the long course of history. Even under the rule of the authoritarian regime, Chinese people still have sincere desire and aspiration for freedom and equality.

> Determined by China's own characteristics, the freedom in the eyes of the contemporary Chinese people is not the "absolute freedom" without any constraint, boundary and condition, but the one showing the rational pursuit and imbued with the scientific value, which is the organic unity of freedom and discipline.

However, the values in the minds and hearts of the contemporary Chinese people are linked and cannot be separated with the real situation of Chinese society. Once they break away from the tradition, national conditions and reality of China, all of them will be nothing but castles in the air, or nothing more than fantasies. Therefore, determined by China's own characteristics, the freedom in the eyes of the contemporary Chinese people is not the "absolute freedom" without any constraint, boundary and condition, but the one showing the rational pursuit and imbued with the scientific value, which is the organic unity of freedom and discipline. The so-called equality in the eyes of contemporary Chinese people has been no longer the egalitarianism that advocates the past blind pursuit of "equality in all", nor the false equality just as a slogan. For contemporary Chinese people, the view of social democracy in pursuit of freedom and equality is a real state that meets the mental and physical needs of man and achieves the organic unity with the outside world, as well as an objective fact that is combined with the real existence and development goals of the Chinese society and Chinese people.

Under the influence of the reform and opening up as well as globalization, the contemporary Chinese people's understanding of freedom, equality and democracy, in fact, has already exceeded the Western society's understanding of Chinese people and Chinese society. Nevertheless, the contemporary Chinese people should creatively establish their own values of freedom, equality and democracy on the basis of the understanding of those in Western society, which still needs time and great efforts. Only when the Chinese people get rid of the intervention of external values and create, establish and really enjoy a view of free and equal socialist democracy of their own and with Chinese characteristics, can they really obtain freedom, equality and democracy.

## 3. A View of Healthy and Positive Social Morality

In recent years, along with China's economic and social development as well as the enhancement of overall national strength, the material life of the Chinese people has been significantly improved. When the standard and quality of material life are improved to a certain degree, people's attention began to turn to the spiritual life. Thereupon, today, many Chinese people start to pay attention to the social cultural life and moral life and take the improvement of the quality of their spiritual life as an important goal. In this case, the status and level of people's social morality has become an important topic for discussion, and issues of social morality have also become a concern of many people. However, the social events that spread under the modern information-based conditions often call people's attention to issues of social morality.

Among those people who pay attention to issues of social morality, there are two diametrically opposed views on the moral condition of the Chinese people since the reform and opening up: one view argues that since the reform and opening up the moral condition of the Chinese people has deteriorated, moral decline is serious and moral anomie has been close to the bottom line of social ethics. In recent years there have been a lot of events that can be used by people who hold this view to illustrate the moral decline and moral degeneration. For example, in 2006, there was a quite confusing case in Nanjing city—Peng Yu case, the main role of this case Peng Yu was sued because he helped an old woman who fell down, but the old woman claimed that it was Peng Yu who knocked her down and asked for compensation. Due to the intervention of the media and people's ignorance of the truth of the event, the case seems to be complicated and confusing all the time. However, many people, especially netizens, finally believed that Peng Yu was wronged. From this case, people generally feel that the social morality and ethical trust of the contemporary Chinese people are in crisis. And it seems that many other following events also enhanced their feeling of this. For example, the "Running Fan" event that occurred during the Wenchuan earthquake in 2008 aroused heated discussion and great repercussions, the notorious event of "charging for corpses" occurred in the south in 2010, and the shocking "Little Yue Yue" event occurred in Guangdong in 2011.

The other view holds that although there are a variety of unhealthy moral phenomena in real life, and even some once-extinct bad moral behavior re-emerges, many new issues also arise; generally speaking, the moral standard of the Chinese people has been greatly improved. The reform and opening up helps Chinese people get rid of the old bad morality and obtain the new morality that adapts to the new age. In this regard, there are also many events in recent years that are enough to be sufficient evidence. For example, the "Modern-day Lei Feng" Guo Mingyi who are enthusiastic in helping others and makes voluntary blood donation all along over many years, the "Most Beautiful Mom" Wu Juping, who caught a baby falling from a high-rise with her own hands in Hangzhou in 2011, the "Most Beautiful Teacher" Zhang Lili, the "Most Beautiful Driver" Wu Bing and so on. In the past few years, "most beautiful" has almost become a buzzword in news reporting, and there are a variety of "most beautiful" phenomena and characters around the country. "Most beautiful" has become a byword for the new morality in China, which conveys people's hope for the various moral phenomena in the contemporary Chinese society and represents the moral ethos in the new era.

"The Most Beautifuls" represent contemporary moral of the Chinese

The contemporary China is in a period of social transformation, and when socialist market economy has preliminarily formed but not yet become mature, it is not only normal but also inevitable that there appears great turmoil, differentiation and change in the fields of thought, culture and morality. Then, what is the intrinsic value pursuit of the contemporary Chinese people in respect of social morality? And have the Chinese people already fallen into the moral abyss as the pessimists said? In our opinion, if people can have an objective and accurate grasp of the real condition of China as well as the development stage of Chinese society, and observe the state of social morality in the contemporary China from the historical and world perspective, it is not difficult to draw an objective and realistic conclusion, that is, the contemporary Chinese people are confronted with a situation of creating new morality and there are phenomena of moral anomie in some areas. But it is over-exaggerated to say that the moral standard of the Chinese people has dropped to a historic low and has been incorrigible.

There is an important point of observation that cannot be ignored in the judgment of the moral condition of a society, that is, when a society no longer tolerates the immoral events in a particular stage of its development, it is just going to meet with a moral progress and sublimation. In contemporary China, people especially young people pass judgment on the occurred events through network every day, and there are voices of both praise and criticism. What they praise are exactly the events in line with virtues and social morals; what they criticize are exactly the evil social events that they wish and try hard to change. The crux of the matter lies not so much as in the large amount of criticism as their starting point that is kind, virtuous, goodness-oriented and good at self-education.

The moral orientation of the contemporary Chinese people is healthy and positive, which glorifies the true, the good and the beautiful and denounces the false, the bad and the ugly. The reason for this is that the contemporary China is in a period of rapid social development and progress, the prosperity in economy, the stability in politics and the openness in society will inevitably require and appeal for a good moral life. Whenever a good deed is done in the society, people will approve and recognize it from the heart and wish for more good deeds, and they are also willing to do good deeds by themselves and will not go against the basic moral standards; whereas when an event contrary to good morals occurred in the society, people are able to detest and reject it from the heart and know that they should educate, admonish and encourage themselves. Then, isn't a moral condition like this exactly a healthy and positive one that is admirable and desirable?

## 4. A View of Coordinated and Progressive Social Stability

"Governing a big country is like cooking a small fish". Compared with any contemporaneous country in the history, China can be regarded as a big country, for it is not only vast in territory, but also large in population, moreover its economy and society are well-developed and the level of civilization is relatively high. The development and progress of a big country requires stability, not only the stability in policy and political course, but also in social environment. From a historical perspective, we can see that the pursuit of stability is the management objective of the rulers of all dynasties in China, and of course, it is also the desire of the ordinary people.

Throughout the development of human society, "governing in stability and changing in disorder" is an important law in it. When the social development is in a state of stability, social governance is relatively easy, and thereby the society as a whole will progress in a more balanced and fair manner; whereas when the society undergoes change, although it, in a certain sense, may bring about social progress and innovation, the cost of the change will be very heavy, and sometimes even become "too heavy to bear" for an era or for a number of groups. In most cases, social stability is most beneficial to the ordinary people, which is one of the reasons why the majority of people, especially the general people, hope that the society can be stable in the long term.

Among the value judgments about the society held by the Chinese people, the view of stability is one of the core values. In order to win stability, feudal rulers made all efforts and used all means, such as establishing ethical code, enforcing law, practicing benevolent government, implementing policy of benevolence, treasuring labor, caring about people's livelihood, winning over and conciliating opponents, and controlling and quelling disturbances. Under the guidance of feudal policy, people stressed discipline, followed etiquette, maintained reputation and integrity, valued harmony, and took the stable order of production and life as one of the most important values. Until today, the Chinese people still maintain the habit of seeking stability in their daily life. For the sake of stability, they emphasize harmony and detest war, and they carry out reform or get themselves into war only as the last resort. Even today, such sayings as "stability overrides everything", "stability is the biggest political task", "development can be realized only in stability", and "no trouble making" are still very important ideas of governing a state, and behind these modern sayings, it is the same values of the pursuit of stability that are contained in them.

However, it is also known that although stability is conducive to the consolidation, it may also lead to rigidity sometimes. It is not enough for the development of society to only rely on stability, it still needs positive changes, through which it can obtain vitality and energy. Taking a brief look at Chinese history, we will find that there are changes in almost all dynasties; especially, whenever the society gets too rigid or loses the force of development, some people will come out to promote the change, such as the Reforms of Shang Yang in the Qin Dynasty, the Reforms of Wang An-shih in the Northern Song Dynasty, and the Wu Hsu Reform in late Qing. Indeed, the change may bring about temporary and local unrest, but ultimately, it will be also conducive to the stability and sustainable development of the society.

> Only if a high level of coordination between stability and change is reached, can a good result of development be produced.

To deal well with the relationship between change and stability is the key to achieving the effective social development. In Chinese history, many dynasties actively or passively adopt means of reform to govern the country and manage state affairs. However, just because some of them did not deal well with the relationship between change and stability, their regimes come to an end. Change and stability fall into a dialectical category, which represent the two sides of the coin of social existence and development, and neither of the sides can be biased or neglected. Only by coordinating the relationship between change and stability well and seeking an optimal state between them, can we achieve the sound government, the best stability and development. Therefore, only if a high level of coordination between stability and change is reached, can a good result of development be produced.

In order to obtain the stable development and coordinated progress of the society, rulers of China are accustomed to using two means of governance: the rule of morality and the rule of law. There have been the tradition of Legalism and the dynasties that took Legalism as their idea of state governance in Chinese history, among which the Qin Dynasty is a dynasty like this. However, after the Qin and Han dynasties, Confucianism became flourishing and gradually occupied a dominant position in the ideas of state governance, thereupon in more than two thousand years, China was under the strong influence of Confucianism. Thus, in the system of social values of the Chinese, the importance of the rule of law and the legal system are set aside. During the long-term feudal rule, the rule of morality advocated by Confucianism became orthodox idea, and the principle of mainly relying on morality supplemented by penalty became the basic standards for social governance in China. In people's minds, heavy penalty and severe law provide for a behavioral limit that they cannot exceed, while the cultivation of morality is their value pursuit that they have taken for granted. In fact, social stability, to a great extent, relies on people's moral cultivation.

Today, Chinese people are sparing no effort to promote the cause of socialism with Chinese characteristics, and it is not enough to rely solely on either of the means of the rule of morality and the rule of law in the process of building the socialist market economy, socialist democratic politics and socialist advanced culture. More and more Chinese people began to view the relationships between change and stability, the rule of morality and the rule of law from a dialectical perspective. More and more people come to realize that the social development requires both stability and change. Whether in stability or in change, the progress of China requires both the rule of morality and the rule of law, moreover, only when the two realize the organic integration and effective complementation, can the society be coordinated and promoted. The contemporary Chinese people neither abandon the excellent tradition of the rule of morality nor reject the scientific idea of the rule of law. In their minds, the rule of morality and the rule of law have been promoted to the equally important position, and stability and change have had the equally important value.

**Notes**

[1] The speech at the welcome meeting of business circles and various parties in Shanxi (September 20, 1912), See *The Collected Works of Sun Yat-sen*, Volume 2, Beijing: Zhonghua Book Company, 1982, p. 476.

[2] "Plans for National Reconstruction • Sun Wen Theory" (1917—1919), See *The Collected Works of Sun Yat-sen*, Volume 6, Beijing: Zhonghua Book Company, 1985, p. 210.

**图书在版编目（CIP）数据**

中国人的价值观：英文/宇文利著；张兴权译. —北京：中国人民大学出版社，2012.11

（“认识中国·了解中国”书系）

ISBN 978-7-300-16671-1

Ⅰ.①中… Ⅱ.①宇…②张… Ⅲ.①人生观-研究-中国-英文 Ⅳ.①B82

中国版本图书馆CIP数据核字（2012）第269528号

“认识中国·了解中国”书系

**中国人的价值观**

宇文利 著

张兴权 译

| | | | |
|---|---|---|---|
| **出版发行** | 中国人民大学出版社 | | |
| **社　　址** | 北京中关村大街31号 | **邮政编码** | 100080 |
| **电　　话** | 010－62511242（总编室） | | 010－62511398（质管部） |
| | 010－82501766（邮购部） | | 010－62514148（门市部） |
| | 010－62515195（发行公司） | | 010－62515275（盗版举报） |
| **网　　址** | http://www.crup.com.cn | | |
| | http://www.ttrnet.com（人大教研网） | | |
| **经　　销** | 新华书店 | | |
| **印　　刷** | 北京鑫丰华彩印有限公司 | | |
| **规　　格** | 170 mm×250 mm　16开本 | **版　　次** | 2012年12月第1版 |
| **印　　张** | 11.5 插页2 | **印　　次** | 2012年12月第1次印刷 |
| **字　　数** | 134 000 | **定　　价** | 138.00元 |